CLASH

ALSO BY THE SAME AUTHOR

Marketing as Strategy: Understanding the CEO's Agenda for Driving Growth and Innovation (Boston: Harvard Business School Press, 2004)

Global Marketing: 10 Selected Case Studies (New Delhi: Businessworld, 2006)

Private Label Strategy: How to Meet the Store Brand Challenge (Nirmalya Kumar and Jan-Benedict Steenkamp, Boston: Harvard Business School Press, 2007)

Value Merchants: Demonstrating and Documenting Superior Value in Business Markets (James C. Anderson, Nirmalya Kumar and James A. Narus, Boston: Harvard Business School Press, 2007)

India's Global Powerhouses: How They Are Taking on the World (Nirmalya Kumar, Pradipta K. Mohapatra and Suj Chandrasekhar, Boston: Harvard Business School Press, 2009)

India Inside: The Emerging Innovation Challenge to the West (Nirmalya Kumar and Phanish Puranam, Boston: Harvard Business Press, 2012)

Brand Breakout: How Emerging Market Brands Will Go Global (Nirmalya Kumar and Jan-Benedict Steenkamp, London: Palgrave Macmillan, 2013)

Thinking Smart: How to Master Work, Life and Everything In-Between (New Delhi: HarperCollins India, 2018)

Hemen Mazumdar: The Last Romantic (Caterina Corni and Nirmalya Kumar, Singapore: Singapore Management University, 2019)

ADVANCE PRAISE FOR THE BOOK

'Dive into the retail battleground where Amazon's digital prowess clashes with Walmart's brick-and-mortar might. Nirmalya Kumar unveils the strategic dance between the e-commerce giant and the retail titan, offering fresh perspectives and counter-intuitive insights into their contrasting paths to dominance'—Harsh Mariwala, chairman, Marico and Kaya Limited

'Walmart (the incumbent leader in offline retailing) and Amazon (the attacking leader in online retailing) make up the most interesting business drama of our times. Will each stick to its current leadership role or will they emerge as dominant players in both roles? Nirmalya Kumar offers the best study that I have seen of these two world-wrestling competitors'—Philip Kotler, S.C. Johnson & Son Distinguished Professor of International Marketing, Kellogg School of Management, Northwestern University

'This remarkable book covers the clash between Walmart and Amazon and then uses that backdrop to decode the evolution of the consumer shopping experience, from retail and e-commerce to omnichannel. Professor Nirmalya Kumar at his insightful best!'—Inderpal Bhandari, independent director, Walgreens Boots Alliance, and former global chief data officer, IBM

CLASH

Amazon vs Walmart

NIRMALYA KUMAR

PENGUIN
BUSINESS

An imprint of Penguin Random House

PENGUIN BUSINESS

USA | Canada | UK | Ireland | Australia
New Zealand | India | South Africa | China | Singapore

Penguin Business is part of the Penguin Random House group of companies
whose addresses can be found at global.penguinrandomhouse.com

Published by Penguin Random House India Pvt. Ltd
4th Floor, Capital Tower 1, MG Road,
Gurugram 122 002, Haryana, India

Penguin
Random House
India

First published in Penguin Business by Penguin Random House India 2024

10 9 8 7 6 5 4 3 2 1

ISBN 9780143466529

Typeset in Sabon by Manipal Technologies Limited, Manipal
Printed at Thomson Press India Ltd, New Delhi

www.penguin.co.in

In memory of Cyrus P. Mistry, who

- *Gave me an opportunity that no one else would have,*
- *Allowed me to publicly disagree, which no chairman/ promoter would have,*
- *Taught me some things you can only learn from a clash.*

You left too early, my friend—I miss you!

Contents

Preface

My interest in retailing began during my PhD programme. My dissertation adviser, Louis W. Stern, guided me towards research on marketing channels. Retailing was a large and critical element of this research programme. In 1994, I started teaching the Harvard Business School case study on Walmart. This case, which I must have taught 500 times perhaps, and finally retired in 2022, became a mainstay of my presentations in degree programmes, executive education and consulting gigs. Over the years, I also wrote at least three cases each on Amazon and Walmart. As such, this book has been simmering in my head for three decades.

In 1996, with my good friend and colleague Jacques Horovitz, who sadly passed away, we launched a retail programme at International Institute for Management Development (IMD). This programme was instrumental in my education in retailing, especially of European and Asian retailers. To support my teaching and research on the topic, I authored case studies on many retail and e-commerce firms, including Aldi (2007), Carrefour (1998), Foodworld (1997), Gucci (2021), LeShop (2003), Online Grocery Retailing (2000), Priceline (2001),

Starbucks (2019), the UK supermarket industry (1996) and Zara (2005, 2018).

The research conducted on retailing was academically productive. It resulted in the book, *Private Label Strategy* (co-authored with J-B Steenkamp in 2007), which has become the default text on private labels and is used by retailers in India to set up their private label programmes. I was also fortunate to author several articles related to retailing in *Harvard Business Review*, beginning with my first article on creating trust in manufacturer–retailer relationships in 1996. Subsequent to that were *Harvard Business Review* articles on the adoption of efficient consumer response (ECR) and rationalizing brand portfolios in response to retailer power in 2003, strategies to fight low-cost retailers in 2006, and the rise of hard discounters in 2009. More academic contributions on managing manufacturer–retailer relationships appeared in the *Academy of Management Journal* (2003), the *International Journal of Research in Marketing* (1996, 1998), the *Journal of Marketing* (effects of ECR in 2005) and the *Journal of Marketing Research* (several articles in 1992, 1995, 1998, 1999 and 2001).

The institutional backbone this book rests on are the many consulting assignments for retailers and brand manufacturers in their quest to effectively manage operations. Retail clients have included the Aditya Birla Group, Auchan, Bata, Bertelsmann, C&A, Jardine Matheson, Jerónimo Martins, Raymond and Sonae. Particularly enlightening was the opportunity to advise Foodworld Supermarkets, starting from the 1996 launch of their first store in Bangalore (now Bengaluru), India. As they scaled up, Pradipta Mohapatra and Raghu Pillai (both unfortunately now deceased), their then CEOs, and I met regularly to train the executives to improve operations. The alumni of Foodworld subsequently went on to take up leading executive roles in the exploding Indian modern retail industry. During my stint as strategy head of the Tata Group, I served on the boards of Tata Chemicals and Tata Unistore and also interacted with the Tata retail companies Croma, Starbucks, Tanishq and Titan.

The brand manufacturers seeking help with their retail and distribution strategy are too numerous to mention. However, repeat clients included AkzoNobel, Caterpillar, Coca-Cola, Danone, Ford Motors, Hewlett Packard, Holcim, IBM, Lego, Nestlé, LVMH, Procter & Gamble, Sara Lee, Sony, Telenor, Toyota, TUI and Unilever. It has been a wonderful learning journey over thirty years as retailing is a constantly evolving and exciting industry. As a result of these experiences, this book, I hope, is valuable to readers.

I have been fortunate to have had meaningful discussions about retailing with Bob Blattberg and (the late) Doug Tigert as well as on Indian retailing with Atul Singh, who headed Coca-Cola South Asia; Devndra Chawla, who held CEO/leadership positions at Future Group, Nature's Basket, Spencer's and Walmart India; Kishore Biyani of Future Group; Noel Tata; and Thomas Varghese, who led More Retail. It has been my privilege to collaborate with amazing academics over the years: Caterina Corni, Daniel Corsten, Harish Sujan, Inge Geyskens, (the late) Jacques Horovitz, James Narus, Jan-Benedict Steenkamp, (the late) Jean-Philippe Deschamps, James Anderson, Jonathan Hibbard, Koen Pauwels, Lisa Scheer, Louis W. Stern, Madan Pillutla, Marco Bertini, Palash Deb, Phanish Puranam, Philip Kotler, Prothit Sen, Ravi Achrol and (the late) Thomas Vollmann. They taught me much.

1

Amazon and Walmart on a
Collision Course

Once upon a time, in the bustling town of Retailville, there was a row of quaint and charming shops. Each shop was unique, offering a variety of goods and services that catered to the diverse needs and tastes of the townspeople. For years, these local retailers flourished, enjoying the trust and loyalty of their customers. When Retailville shoppers wanted more choice, sophisticated products or an upscale experience, they headed to the nearest metropolis, where they were overwhelmed by options ranging from large heritage retailers such as JCPenney, Kmart, Lord & Taylor and Sears, and aspirational department stores such as Barneys New York and Neiman Marcus, to pioneering category killers such as Borders, Circuit City, Radio Shack and Toys "R" Us. However, change was on the horizon.

Beginning from humble origins in Bentonville, Arkansas, Walmart began putting large physical stores with discounted prices into little one-horse towns like Retailville, which everyone else was ignoring. Walmart's 'one-stop shop' approach enticed many townspeople, who were drawn to the promise of finding everything they needed under one roof. The existing retailers, especially mom-and-pop stores, began to feel the heat as customers diverted their attention and wallets to Walmart.

Just as Walmart seemed to have become unstoppable, a new entity, Amazon, emerged. Amazon, whose digital marketplace offered a wide array of products delivered right to customers' doorsteps. With the convenience of online shopping and an ever-expanding selection, Amazon quickly gained popularity among the townspeople.

As time went on, the shopkeepers noticed a change in their foot traffic. Once-bustling streets grew quieter and the jingle of the cash registers became less frequent. The allure of the giants' convenience and competitive prices proved irresistible to many, and the retailers found themselves struggling to keep up.

The shopkeepers held a meeting in the town square, worried about the uncertain future that lay ahead. Caterina, the owner of a charming bookstore, spoke up with concern. 'We've always prided ourselves on the personal touch we bring to our businesses,' she said. 'But now, people seem to prefer the ease of clicking a button or rushing through aisles.' Harry, who ran a family-owned electronics store, added, 'We must find a way to remind our customers of the value we bring—the relationships we've built, the expertise we offer and the sense of community we create.' But the evidence from the larger towns was ominous. Each of the large retailers aforementioned had been forced into bankruptcy by the onslaught of Amazon and Walmart!

Could the town of Retailville thrive, not by competing on the giants' terms, but by nurturing the spirit of community and personal touch that made local businesses an indispensable part of the town's identity? Moreover, could the remaining larger retailers prevail in the face of seemingly insurmountable challenges through innovation, exceptional customer experience and distinctive propositions? Or should they find solace in the rise of the omnichannel shopper? Were Amazon and Walmart themselves headed towards an unavoidable fatal confrontation, where only a single winner would emerge from the clash?

The Two Most Successful Retailers in History

With sales of $611 billion in 2022, Walmart continued its dominance as the world's largest company by revenue, a position that it first achieved in 2002.[1] In contrast, the e-commerce pioneer Amazon, founded only in 1997 and with revenues of $514 billion in 2022, became, for the first time, the world's second-largest corporation.[2] The surge in online shopping over 2020–21, on account of the COVID-19 global pandemic, had enabled the e-retailer to considerably shrink the gap from Walmart.

Although Walmart led Amazon in revenues as well as in operating income (at $20.4 billion versus Amazon at $12.2 billion) in 2022, on 17 November 2023, Amazon's $1.5 trillion valuation dwarfed the $418 billion market capitalization of Walmart. Clearly, the markets appreciated the business model and growth prospects of Amazon over Walmart. One can imagine that despite higher sales and profitability than Amazon, Walmart's market cap being less than a third of Amazon's market cap is a source of frustration to Walmart's top management.

The perceived market 'disrespect' is symbolic of a larger narrative, where traditional incumbent firms are not considered as 'sexy' as new-age disruptors, even when the latter have lower revenues and marginal, if any, profitability. Think Tesla or Uber versus the incumbent automakers and car rental companies as well as Airbnb or OYO versus leading hotel chains. However, the 'age of the unicorns' (start-ups with billion dollar-plus valuations) is a relatively recent phenomenon. Prior to 2003, even successful digital disruptors like Google did not command such valuations as private companies. Therefore, Amazon versus Walmart has great resonance for incumbents in general as they confront the challenge of digital transformation and combat new entrants with disruptive business models. Often, incumbents view these new business models with suspicion (refer to Table 1.1 for a comparison of the retailers' sales, operating income and market capitalization).

Table 1.1. Financial Overview of Amazon and Walmart

	Financial Year*	Worldwide Revenues	Operating Income	Market Capitalization**
Amazon	2022	514.0	12.2	856.9
	2012	61.1	0.7	113.9
	2002	3.9	0.1	7.3
Walmart	2022	611.3	20.4	382.4
	2012	469.2	27.8	228.2
	2002	246.5	13.6	223.4

* Amazon financial year ends 31 December; Walmart financial year ends 31 January of the following year.
** As on 31 December of the year. Numbers are in billions of US dollars.
Source: Amazon.com Inc. and Walmart Inc. Annual Reports.

As the two most successful retailers in history, Amazon and Walmart have transformed the retail industry by redefining customer orientation, supplier-retailer relationships and the use of information technology. Both retailers have leveraged their tremendous power over suppliers to offer the lowest prices possible to consumers. Historically, the two firms did not compete directly against each other because of their differing focus. While Walmart dominated the 'slow-growing' brick-and-mortar retail that comprised approximately 85 per cent of the US retail industry, Amazon led the 'fast-growing' e-commerce sector that contributed the remaining 15 per cent in 2022.[3]

Over the years, the two firms had optimized contrasting business models to enable their dominance of offline and online retailing, respectively. Walmart's model was based on offering the lowest prices on everyday goods for its in-store shoppers through a vast store network. The retailer had redefined supply chain practices and lowered system costs by developing strategic partnerships with its largest suppliers and leading the adoption of information technology. In contrast, Amazon's online model was based on offering the convenience of shopping from anywhere, anytime. It focused on developing a user-friendly platform that comprised a 600-million-plus product catalogue and a widespread and reliable fulfilment infrastructure to deliver orders quickly. The success of these two retailers was reflected in the fact that in 2022, 95 per cent of all US consumers had shopped at a Walmart store while 71 per cent had shopped at Amazon.[4]

However, the growing consumer preference for omnichannel retailing, an integrated experience that seamlessly comprised digital and physical retail, compelled the two companies to make substantive investments in developing capabilities and acquiring resources in what was hitherto the other's domain.

Since 2015, Walmart increasingly reduced its spending on opening new stores, and instead, focused more on e-initiatives that facilitated online retail, such as the launch of pick-up towers, expansion of grocery delivery locations, adoption of technology and a supply chain that supported an omnichannel model, besides remodelling existing stores to make them more attractive to shoppers. In 2016, Walmart acquired Jet.com, an innovative e-commerce company in the US, for $3.3 billion, and retained its highly experienced leader, Marc Lore, as the CEO of Walmart's e-commerce business. This was followed by a $18 billion acquisition of India's leading online retailer, Flipkart, in 2018. As a result of these efforts, Walmart became the leading competitor of Amazon in online sales in the US (refer to Table 1.2 for retailers' online market shares). In 2022, Walmart's online operations exceeded $82 billion in sales, of which $54.4 billion, $20.3 billion and $8.4 billion were from North America, international and Sam's Club respectively.

Table 1.2. Leading Retail E-commerce Companies in the US

Retailer	% Share 2022
Amazon	37.8%
Walmart	6.3%
Apple	3.9%
eBay	3.5%
Target	2.1%
The Home Depot	2.1%
Best Buy	1.8%
Costco	1.6%
Carvana	1.5%
Kroger	1.4%

Source: Stephanie Chevalier, 'Leading Retail Online Companies in the US,' Statista, 10 July 2023, https://www.statista.com/statistics/274255/market-share-of-the-leading-retailers-in-us-e-commerce, accessed August 2023.

Concurrently, Amazon started investing in creating an offline presence by establishing a variety of access points to provide shoppers with a physical browsing experience. Between 2015 and 2021, it opened twenty-four bookstores across the US.[5] It also rolled out eighty-seven pop-up stores/kiosks, which housed an assortment of Amazon hardware products. However, the pop-up concept did not resonate with customers and the company decided to discontinue them. More substantially, in 2017, Amazon acquired Whole Foods, a premium grocery chain with 470 stores, for $13.7 billion. By 2022, Amazon decided to concentrate on Whole Foods Market, Amazon Fresh (food and groceries) stores and Amazon Style (apparel) stores, having generated $19 billion in revenues from its 500-plus physical stores in 2022.

The battle between Amazon and Walmart is a bellwether for the retail industry. The rise of online shopping, accelerated by the outbreak of COVID-19, had large, famous retailers with storied pasts, such as Barneys New York, Circuit City, Forever21, JCPenney, Kmart, Macy's, Neiman Marcus, Pier 1 Imports, Sears and Toys "R" Us, forced into the liquidation process. Unable to emerge from Chapter 11, some like A&P, Blockbuster, Borders and Radio Shack disappeared completely from the retail landscape. As the retail apocalypse continued in 2020, a record 12,200 stores closed in the US.[6] Clearly, brick-and-mortar retailers were facing an existential crisis, unable to meet the digital transformation challenge or the competition from the juggernauts, Amazon and Walmart.

The Rise of E-commerce

The history of e-commerce can be divided into roughly three stages. The first, in the 1990s, commonly referred to as the 'dot-com bubble', saw start-up online players, primarily from Silicon Valley, on a gold rush. This speculative phase ended in March 2000, when many young Internet companies that had been rushed into IPOs with low revenues and high operating losses went bust.

The first decade of the millennium represented the second stage of e-commerce. While a few survivors from the first phase, having stabilized their online business models, re-emerged in Silicon Valley, the second e-commerce centre of gravity was established in China. Baidu, Alibaba and Tencent, sometimes referred to as BAT, benefited from the large Chinese market with an underdeveloped physical retail infrastructure and strong protection of the domestic market to build some of the most valuable firms in the world. Learning from the mistakes of the US-based start-ups during the dot-com bubble, their innovations in products, processes and business models represented global best practices for e-commerce and generated high profitability. As a result, the market capitalization of Alibaba and Tencent rivalled that of Meta, all within $600–700 billion at one stage in 2022, despite the limited global footprint of the Chinese companies.

While most traditional retail firms watched warily or experimented gingerly with online sales in the first two stages of e-commerce, the decade of 2010–2020 converted even the most rabid non-believers. Interestingly, in parallel, pioneering e-commerce players like Amazon and Alibaba began to appreciate the limits of an online-only model. Instead of ignoring each other, both traditional and online retailers were increasingly betting that the future of retail lay in the smart combination of physical stores with online presence, or what is known as omnichannel retailing.

For traditional retailers, being omnichannel can be as basic as just adding a website for click-and-collect from the store, which requires little transformation and offers only an additional order-taking platform to customers. At the other end of the spectrum, it can be a fully integrated offline-online presence, such as Tesco has in the UK, allowing all combinations of ordering and delivery. A customer can shop at the store in the traditional manner, or order online for delivery at home, or shop in-store and request home delivery, or even click and collect. Through its loyalty programme, Tesco recognizes, rewards and responds to customers, no matter where they may start and end their shopping journey.

On the other hand, online retailers like Alibaba and Amazon are setting up their own stores as well as acquiring existing brick-and-mortar chains to add to their physical footprint. Beyond this, e-commerce players are seeking physical presence through existing retailer networks. For example, if you wish to return a product to Amazon in the US or the UK, the company asks you to print out a label and attach it to the package, which can then be left at a designated convenience store in your neighbourhood. In China, some large home and office buildings have installed lockers in common areas where deliveries can be left unattended. The customer is sent a unique code on their mobile phone to unlock and collect their order.

Online sales already account for 15–20 per cent of retail sales in major markets such as China, the UK and the US. While the COVID-19 pandemic in 2020 accelerated the retail migration from offline to online, in 2021, the US surprisingly reported net store openings, a sudden reversal from years of net store declines, as customers returned to stores (refer to Table 1.3 for online retail history). Yet, this is most likely a one-off blip owing to the reopening of stores as the pandemic abated—40,000 to 50,000 retail stores are still expected to be shuttered in the US by 2026.[7]

With Walmart and Amazon racing to add online and offline retail, respectively, will their distinctive business models morph to become like each other? Or will each focus on its core strength while offering the other service (online for Walmart and offline for Amazon) as complementary? In other words, are the two retail giants headed for a direct head-on clash or will they coexist with strategic complementarity? Do the respective prospects of Amazon and Walmart truly justify the dramatic differences in market capitalization between the two retailers? This book grapples with these questions and utilizes the ensuing discussion to investigate the implications for the rest of the retail industry.

Walmart facing Amazon is also a microcosm of the traditional retail industry grappling with incontrovertible

Table 1.3. Total and E-commerce Value of US Retail

In	2012	2013	2014	2015	2016	2017	2018	2019	2020	2021	2022
Total retail trade sales in $ billion	4300	4460	4640	4720	4830	5050	5260	5410	5580	6588	7100
Retail e-commerce sales in $ billion	231	261	297	338	383	443	507	570	812	960	1033
E-commerce sales % of total retail	5.4	5.8	6.4	7.2	7.9	8.8	9.6	10.5	14.6	14.6	14.6

Source: Data from Oberlo, 'US Retail Sales', https://www.oberlo.com/statistics/us-retail-sales; and Oberlo, 'US E-commerce Sales', https://www.oberlo.com/statistics/us-ecommerce-sales, accessed June 2022.

questions. Which consumers prefer traditional physical stores and for which needs? Are there certain product categories, like groceries compared to electronics, which consumers prefer to buy from the local brick-and-mortar stores? What can brick-and-mortar stores do to slow the loss in their market share to online retailing? How do they make the shopping experience in physical stores more compelling? In addition, as they add online orders to the mix, what is a superior fulfilment strategy—delivery from the nearest store, as Walmart does, or delivery from dedicated warehouses, as Amazon prefers? And, perhaps most importantly, will online sales be profit-accretive or earnings-dilutive (online sales are less profitable than physical store sales) for traditional incumbent retailers?

Plan of the Book

Chapter 2 documents the birth and rise of Walmart, the original disruptor of the retail industry and one of the world's most hallowed companies in the 1980s and 1990s. A feared competitor and customer with a distinctive counter-intuitive business model, Walmart was the benchmark for best practices. An early adopter of information technology for running the business, it also revolutionized how retailers managed their relationships with manufacturers. Over the past ten years, the retailer has made substantial investments in online retail to become the leading competitor to Amazon. While it may be currently fashionable to write off brick-and-mortar retailers, Walmart is deeply entrenched and continues to grow with sustained profitability.

Chapter 3 follows the rise of Amazon from a start-up in the e-commerce space to becoming the dominant online retailer in the US, and increasingly in the world, except for China. Amazon's risk-taking culture has transformed, what was initially conceptualized as retailing books online, into retailing everything online. But, more impressively, and beyond any initial imagination of its founder, Jeff Bezos, Amazon has continuously innovated into new arenas including cloud computing, third-party marketplace, content creation, devices, physical stores, property development and advertising. As a result, depending on the day of assessment, Amazon is the world's most valuable brand and most valuable company, making Jeff Bezos the richest man globally. Amazon is a remarkable example of a firm continuously pivoting its business model, building new capabilities and redefining its key success factors.

Chapter 4 dives into understanding the needs of target consumers and the value proposition of online versus offline retail. While, yes, the decline of physical stores is a result of consumers increasingly moving online and the overall picture for offline retailing does not look promising, a more nuanced view is warranted. Specifically, under what buying situations do physical stores remain a powerful proposition for shoppers? What insights can be gained from examining three product categories where the online penetration of category sales differ substantially: groceries, apparel and books/music, with approximately 5–10 per cent, 35–40 per cent and 65–70 per cent of total category sales, respectively, being generated online? What are the consumer, product and retail drivers behind this variation in online penetration? It is anticipated that this discussion will help any retailer or manufacturer to reflect on their own future mix of online and physical distribution.

Chapter 5 examines the profitability of Amazon, and more generally, online retailing. Among the questions explored, a significant one is: Does Amazon generate any profits from its retail operations? Or does Amazon rely on its cloud computing business (AWS) to subsidize its retail? In general, it was presumed, and perhaps still is by some, that an online retailer like Amazon has considerable financial advantage over brick-and-mortar players like Walmart with respect to less asset intensity (e.g., physical stores, inventory, fittings) and lower operating costs (e.g., staff, utilities). In this chapter, the evolution of delivery costs at Amazon is investigated to assess scale effects. Are delivery costs falling as a percentage of sales as Amazon grows rapidly? What effect does Amazon Prime have on delivery costs? How do the asset and inventory turnover ratios compare across the two retailers? What types of online retailing can be profitable? How should one evaluate the long-term viability of Amazon's model? Is Amazon's profitability now dependent on its ability to mine consumer data for insights?

Chapter 6 describes the different approaches adopted by Amazon and Walmart in fulfilling online orders. Specifically, Walmart uses its vast network of physical stores to ship the product from the nearest store to the customer. In contrast, Amazon has invested heavily in building dedicated warehouses and an associated infrastructure to handle online order fulfilment. What are the benefits and drawbacks of fulfilment via stores versus warehouses in terms of the economics and the scalability? Walmart's efforts in e-commerce and Amazon's continued push to improve the performance and efficiency of delivery are outlined. Both firms, like most online retailers, need to confront how to make consumer returns easy and rare, especially for apparel. Finally, the delivery business, while loved by consumers, is challenging from the profit, people and planet perspectives.

Chapter 7 investigates how traditional brick-and-mortar retailers are meeting the challenge posed by online retail. The physical store is a valuable piece of real estate, but to survive in an e-commerce world, it needs a strong value proposition. Why should the consumer come into a store? Several successful brick-and-mortar retailer strategies are identified. While a rash of bankruptcies has rocked physical retail chains over the past two decades, there are also many examples of thriving store chains, including 7/11, Aldi, Apple, Costco, IKEA, Lidl, lululemon and Zara. Airport duty-free stores continue to grow and malls in the US are making a comeback after decades of decline.

Chapter 8 delves into emerging markets with a focus on India, where, the next big clash between Amazon and Walmart is playing out after North America. While developed markets are overstored, emerging markets are seeing simultaneous growth in online and offline retail. With China out of bounds to Amazon, and Walmart still struggling in the country despite operating there since 1996, India has become the must-win market for both these retailers. They have poured substantial investments into India over the past two decades while struggling to generate any profits. With Walmart's reported sales slightly ahead of Amazon in India, is this the market where Walmart beats Amazon?

Chapter 9 steps back from the specifics of Amazon versus Walmart to examine the general competition between disruptors and incumbents (e.g., Airbnb versus Marriott) that is ubiquitous currently. These two types of firms differ in strategic capabilities, with incumbents excelling at exploitation while the strength of the disruptors is exploration of new arenas. The incumbents follow a profit maximization financial approach while disruptors tend to favour shareholder value maximization. Finally, the incumbents fundamentally have a product-based model that relies on the difference between buying and selling prices. In contrast, the disruptors favour platform models that facilitate interaction between parties.

Conclusion

The retail industry has evolved over centuries as one of the oldest and largest sectors of any economy. It stands as a cornerstone of modern society, its importance transcending mere commerce. At its core, retail revolves around the needs and desires of consumers. It's a domain where convenience meets cost, offering a diverse range of products and services that cater to individuals' everyday lives. This accessibility ensures that retail remains an essential aspect of our society. Historically, leading retailers like Aldi, Lidl, IKEA, Walmart and now even Amazon have, through their brutal efficiency, lowered inflation for consumers, increased consumption and expanded living standards.

In terms of employment, the retail industry is a powerhouse. Historically, retail stores provide large-scale employment, especially entry-level jobs, to unskilled workers at the storefront. But it is sometimes easy to forget that retailers also employ individuals with a wide range of skill sets, from highly skilled merchandisers, digital marketers and IT specialists to managers. As such, retail provides opportunities for people from all walks of life. In the US, retailing is estimated to employ 18 million people. Globally, Amazon and Walmart together account for 4 million employees!

Economically, the retail sector contributes significantly. It facilitates organized finance, creating a structured framework for businesses to operate within. Suppliers also greatly benefit from the retail industry. It forms an integral part of the value chain, ensuring the flow of goods and services from producers to consumers in a cost-effective manner. Retailers create demand, driving production and distribution, which in turn stimulates economic growth.

Moreover, retail often serves as the catalyst for urban centres' development and growth, transforming empty spaces into bustling hubs of activity. The presence of thriving retail businesses can be a key indicator of a region's economic vitality. As main street and high street stores go bankrupt, the role of retail in keeping city centres vibrant as well as the taxes they generate for local communities is garnering greater appreciation.

The retail landscape is constantly evolving, from traditional mom-and-pop stores to the emergence of supermarkets, convenience stores, malls and department stores. These were followed by other innovative retail formats such as discounters, club stores, category killers and hard discounters. This evolution continues today, with the rise of online retail and social commerce. In this ever-changing landscape, retailers must embrace innovation and adapt to the evolving needs of consumers to thrive. Creative destruction is a hallmark of the industry, where old formats lose market share, though they rarely fade away entirely. While the retail industry has traditionally been dominated by relatively small companies from a global standpoint, a landmark shift occurred last year. For the first time in history, two retailers occupied the top two positions on the list of the largest companies in the world.

In summary, the importance of the retail industry extends far beyond its corporate balance sheets, shaping the way we live, work and consume. As physical stores continue to disappear and the last two decades dramatically challenge what is viewed as retail, the implications for economies, people and society cannot be underestimated. The outcome of the battle is unknown: Do both Amazon and Walmart exist in strategic complementarity with the remaining retailers bearing the brunt of their onslaught, does one send the other into oblivion, or does Amazon simply acquire Walmart? Regardless, the clash between Amazon and Walmart has important ramifications and lessons for everybody.

Chapter Takeaways

- Walmart and Amazon, with revenues of $611 and $514 billion, respectively, are the two largest companies in the world. However, Walmart's market cap of around $420 billion is less than a third of Amazon's $1.5 trillion.

- While historically, Amazon focused on online and Walmart on offline retail, they are increasingly morphing into omnichannel players, directly confronting each other. Walmart has built a substantial e-commerce business, while Amazon, through the acquisition of Whole Foods and other experimental formats, has ventured into brick-and-mortar stores. In 2022, Walmart's online sales reached $82 billion, while Amazon's physical stores generated $19 billion.

- The outbreak of the COVID-19 pandemic in 2020 accelerated the adoption of online retail by shoppers. Yet, both 2021 and 2022 saw physical retail bounce back. Walmart grew revenues in 2022, while Amazon's online retail revenues were flat as consumers returned to brick-and-mortar stores. Are the retail giants on a path towards a direct, head-on clash, or are they destined to coexist in strategic complementarity?

2

Walmart: The Original Retail Disruptor

In the bustling landscape of American retail during the 1980s and 1990s, the rise of Walmart had a profound impact on many smaller retailers. One such tale was that of Main Street Treasures, a family-owned variety store that had been a staple of its small town for generations.

Located on the main street of a close-knit community, Main Street Treasures had served as a gathering place where locals could find a diverse range of products, from household essentials to unique gifts. The store was run by the Mittal family, known throughout the town for their friendly demeanour and commitment to quality customer service.

As the 1980s rolled in, a new retail giant named Walmart began to expand its reach across the country. Walmart's promise of 'Everyday Low Prices' and its ability to offer a wide selection of products under one roof proved enticing to many consumers. Main Street Treasures found itself facing a tough challenge as the convenience and affordability of Walmart began to draw customers away.

Despite their dedication and charm, the Mittals found it increasingly difficult to compete with Walmart's economies of scale and aggressive pricing strategies. The store's shelves, once bustling with local products and unique finds, began to seem limited in comparison to the vast aisles of the Walmart supercentre that had opened nearby.

As the 1990s arrived, Main Street Treasures struggled to keep up. The store's loyal customers expressed regret as they explained that they could find similar items at lower prices at Walmart. Over time, foot traffic dwindled, and the Mittals faced difficult decisions about inventory and staffing.

The tale of Main Street Treasures was a poignant example of the challenges many small retailers faced during the rise of Walmart in the 1980s and 1990s. The convenience and low prices that the retail giant offered reshaped consumer expectations and behaviour, leading to the decline of numerous local businesses that simply couldn't compete on the same scale.

While Walmart's expansion brought undeniable benefits to consumers in terms of affordability and convenience, it also prompted a re-evaluation of the value of local businesses and the role they played in creating vibrant and unique communities. The story of Main Street Treasures serves as a reminder of the complex dynamics that accompanied the transformation of the American retail landscape during that era.

The Rise of Walmart

In 1962, Sam Walton opened his first Walmart Discount store in Arkansas, USA. Based on a low-price/high-volume business model, with a vast selection of non-perishables, it expanded into smaller towns and rural areas of the US. Compared to the small mom-and-pop stores at the time, the 30,000 to 80,000 square feet stores, with a greater assortment of products and brands at substantially lower prices, drew shoppers from as far as 50–100 miles away. The strategy of locating stores primarily in towns with a population of 5000 to 25,000 allowed Walmart to benefit from the lower real estate costs (3 per cent of total revenues versus 3.3 per cent of the revenues that direct competitors averaged on rental costs) and limited competition from other big box retailers. It pursued an 'inside-out' radial expansion strategy in locating its stores and warehouses contiguous to existing locations.[1]

The roaring success of the original discount store format over the first twenty-five years (1962–1987) led Walmart to add groceries and perishables via two new store formats, Walmart Supercenters and Sam's Club. Walmart Supercenters were conversions of the original discount stores with additional perishables, especially groceries. Supercenters averaged 1,25,000 square feet, with the largest ones reaching 2,00,000 square feet and 50,000 stock-keeping units (SKUs). In contrast, Sam's Club served small businesses and individuals on a membership basis. They had limited SKUs of around 3500 and sold large pack sizes in a no-frills environment. This enabled Sam's Club to work on lower gross margins of 9–10 per cent compared to the approximately 25 per cent gross margin for Supercenters or discount stores. These new formats required Walmart's supply chain, which had focused on ambient products, to accommodate perishables and chilled products. From the early 1990s onwards, Supercenters and international expansion led Walmart's growth.

In 1998, Walmart enhanced its customer reach by expanding into smaller format stores. Referred to as neighbourhood markets, these were one-fifth the size of Supercenters and primarily stocked food. Conveniently located near urban centres, they offered significantly lower pricing than the local competition. In addition, with e-commerce taking off, the retailer entered the digital space in 2000 through the launch of its website Walmart.com for American consumers to shop online, and followed it up with several 'site-to-store' services that incentivized shoppers to buy online and pick up from its physical stores.

By 2023, Walmart comprised over 10,600 stores globally, serving 230 million customers a week under forty-six banners in over twenty countries and e-commerce websites. Its worldwide sales grew 6.7 per cent in 2022 to $611 billion (refer to Table 2.1 for Walmart's financial performance from 2002 to 2022).[2] In the US, Walmart was the undisputed market leader, with net sales of $508.7 billion for 2022, a growth of 8.2 per cent over the previous year. It had 4600 pickup locations and more than 3900 same-day delivery locations in the country, and its stores and clubs were located within 10 miles of approximately 90 per cent of the US population.

Walmart has been the largest company in the world for the past twenty years, a remarkable achievement for a retailer that, for the most part, still relies on North America for its revenues. One of the most globally admired companies during the 1980s and 1990s, Walmart is an amazing story of a company's rise from humble beginnings. Since the early 2000s, the rise of e-commerce has led physical retail to become unfashionable. As a result, despite dominating the global ranking in terms of revenues, Walmart does not occupy the high pedestal that it once held as a benchmark for business. Yet, it was the original disruptor, with a unique business model. How did a company with a single store in 1962 end up as the largest corporation in the world by 2002? To understand this, one must focus on the original business model, before examining its current evolution into becoming an omnichannel retailer.

Integrated Marketing Strategy

Walmart attracted customers by offering the lowest prices possible, minimizing operating costs and benefiting from

Table 2.1. Walmart Financial Performance

In USD million except for the calculated values	2002	2007	2012	2017	2022
Operating Results					
Net sales	2,46,525	3,78,799	4,69,162	5,00,343	6,11,289
Cost of sales	1,91,838	2,86,515	3,52,488	3,73,396	4,63,721
Operating, SG&A expenses	41,043	70,288	88,873	1,06,510	1,27,140
Operating income	13,644	21,996	27,801	20,437	20,428
Net income	8,232	13,290	17,756	10,523	11,292
Dividends declared per common share ($)	0.30	0.88	1.59	2.04	2.24
Financial Position					
Inventory	25,056	35,180	43,803	43,783	56,576
Property, equipment, capital lease and financing obligation assets, net	51,904	97,017	1,16,681	1,14,818	1,19,234
Total assets	94,685	1,63,514	2,03,105	2,04,522	2,43,197
Return on assets	9.2%	8.4%	9.0%	5.2%	4.6%
Total stockholders' equity	39,337	64,608	76,343	77,869	76,693
Return on equity/investment	21.6%	19.5%	18.2%	14.2%	12.7%
Diluted earnings per share ($)	1.81	3.16	5.02	3.28	4.27
Free cash flow*	NA	5,417	12,693	18,286	11,984

	2002	2007	2012	2017	2022
	Stores Count				
Walmart US segment	2,875	3,550	4,005	4,761	4,717
Walmart international segment	1,288	3,121	6,148	6,360	5,306
Sam's Club segment (US)	525	591	620	597	600
Total count	4,688	7,262	10,773	11,718	10,623
Retail square feet at period end (in millions)*	NA	NA	1,072	1,158	1,056
No. of employees (worldwide)	1,500,000	2,000,000	2,200,000	2,300,000	2,300,000

Financial year end on 31 January of subsequent year; *not available for all the years
Source: Walmart Inc. Annual Reports

economies of scale. In contrast to the 'Hi-Lo' (high regular prices with frequent price promotions) pricing strategy of traditional supermarkets, Walmart offered 'everyday low prices' (EDLP) to all its customers. It included a price-match guarantee, a pricing strategy that was the cornerstone of Walmart's success. Walmart's store managers had the authority to lower the price of any item immediately to meet local competition. On average, Walmart prices were substantially lower, 20–30 per cent lower, than mom-and-pop stores or supermarkets in small towns, and 2–4 per cent lower than its closest big box competitors such as Kmart and Target.

Consistent with EDLP, consumer promotions at Walmart were relatively infrequent, averaging thirteen events annually compared to around fifty to 100 (once or twice weekly) promotion events at other discount stores or supermarkets. Advertising focused on hammering the simple message of 'Always low prices, Always', with Walmart spending considerably less on advertising relative to its direct competitors (1.5 per cent of total revenues versus 2.1 per cent) in the 1990s. The simplicity and focused marketing message combined with increasing scale helped deliver advertising cost efficiencies.

Initially, Walmart focused on selling national manufacturer brands, as it did not have the scale to develop private labels. Over time, it began introducing private labels in the categories where the appropriate price-value combination for shoppers was absent and the opportunity to increase margins existed. Today, Walmart's successful private-label brands include Equate (health and wellness products), Great Value (grocery), Sam's Choice (food products) and Freshness Guaranteed (food products). It also rolled out Uniquely J (coffee, olive oil, laundry detergent and paper towels), which offers quality ingredients at low prices, with bold packaging to attract young customers. Some of the introductions in its private apparel brands portfolio have been Athletic Works (activewear), Time and Tru (women's apparel), Terra & Sky (plus-sized women's clothing), Eloquii (plus-sized women's clothing), Wonder Nation (kids' clothing) and George (men's clothing). It is estimated that 40 per cent of Walmart sales in 2022 were derived from private labels. This would mean an astonishing $250 billion in revenues for Walmart as an own branded company. In contrast, the largest packaged goods branded firms like Nestlé, Johnson & Johnson, PepsiCo and Procter & Gamble had annual revenues of $105 billion, $96 billion, $88 billion and $81 billion, respectively.

Among the large assortment of products Walmart offers, groceries (perishables, frozen foods, beverages, dry groceries, non-perishable household and personal care products) account for the largest share at 56 per cent, followed by general merchandise (entertainment, apparel, home furnishing, stationery, hardware, horticulture, etc.) at 32.3 per cent, and the health and wellness range (pharmacy, optical services, clinical services, over-the-counter drugs and other medical products) at 10.4 per cent.

What made Walmart's customer proposition so compelling was its laser focus on lower prices supported by a disciplined marketing strategy. Unlike most firms that articulate the marketing 4Ps (product, price, place and promotion) individually, Walmart's 4Ps reinforced each other for maximum impact. As Figure 2.1 illustrates, the logic behind the marketing strategy ensured that the 4Ps were not working at cross-purposes.

Most marketing people tend to be very creative when developing the programme for each 'P'. However, this usually results in each 'P' being optimized individually, forgetting the greater marketing strategy behind them as a group. Note that in most firms, pricing strategy is under the supervision of finance, product development is managed by R&D and place or channels are controlled by the sales managers, leaving marketers with

Figure 2.1. Walmart Marketing Strategy

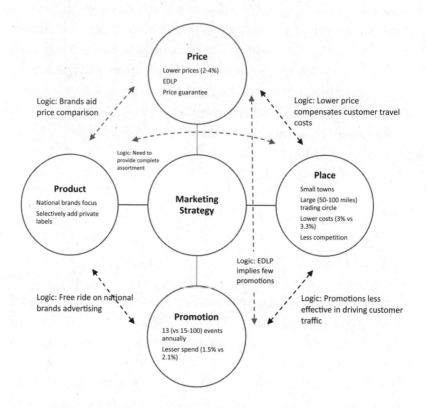

the primary responsibility of promotional activities. To most presentations of marketing strategy, where what they plan to do on each of the 4Ps is presented sequentially, the best retort is—yes, but where is the strategy?

In contrast, Walmart's marketing strategy was mutually reinforcing in the following manner:

- Product*Price: Focus on national brands enables shoppers to compare prices between retailers. For example, Coca-Cola is a commodity from a retailer's perspective as every retailer carries it. However, selling it cheaper than other retailers makes the lower prices of Walmart visible to the shopper. This enables consumers to perceive Walmart's differentiation of low prices. In contrast, for the lower-priced private labels, the customer is never certain if the quality is comparable, muddying the communication of price differential from other retailers.

- Price*Promotion: EDLP pricing strategy implies minimal promotion events. It promises the shopper that the prices offered are the lowest possible across shopping trips. As such, one can shop at Walmart without worrying about it being cheaper on another day, and with the price match guarantee, at another retailer.

- Promotion*Place: If shoppers are driving in from as far as 50 to 100 miles away to reach Walmart, then any individual item on sale will not propel incremental consumer traffic in the same manner as it does for the easily accessible neighbourhood store. The thirteen consumer promotion events annually are mostly to clear out end-of-season merchandise and some widely anticipated sales events like back to school, Thanksgiving or Labour Day sales to encourage shoppers to plan their trips to the store in advance.

- Place*Product: Given the large trading circle, Walmart is a destination store for the consumer's weekly shopping list. It is a hassle (time, costs) to drive to Walmart. If shoppers are unable to find their favourite brand in a particular category upon reaching the store, then the Walmart proposition becomes less powerful as it necessitates a trip to another store to complete the basket. Therefore, Walmart ensures that the store carries a complete assortment of leading manufacturer brands, regardless of its private label strategy.

- Product*Promotion: The focus on national manufacturer brands allows for more efficient advertising. Selling

these brands cheaper allows Walmart to 'free ride' on
the manufacturers' brand advertising and benefit from
consumer word-of-mouth that results from lower prices.
Walmart, therefore, does not need to spend as much on
advertising as the retailers trying to build their own private
labels or run weekly/biweekly promotions that need to be
communicated to potential shoppers.

- Price*Place: Walmart's lower prices are integral to the
  marketing strategy. They incentivize the shopper to travel
  all the way to a Walmart store, bypassing competitors that
  are located closer to them. It compensates the shopper for
  the additional effort, time and costs of reaching a Walmart
  store.

As marketing academics often note, a firm's sales response
function is a summation of the efforts on each of the 4Ps (e.g.,
P1+ P2 + P3 + P4) as well as the interactive effects of the 4Ps
(e.g., P1*P2 + P1*P3 . . . +P1*P2*P3 . . . P1*P2*P3*P4).
Walmart's integrated marketing strategy ensured that the
interactive terms were all positive as the 4Ps reinforced each
other. Unfortunately, in my experience, at many other firms,
the 4Ps either have no positive interaction effects or, even
worse, are in opposition to each other.

Revolutionizing Manufacturer-Retailer Relationships

My 1996 *Harvard Business Review* article, titled 'The Power
of Trust in Manufacturer-Retailer Relationships', documented
how Walmart established strategic partnerships with its
largest vendors, especially Procter & Gamble.[3] To achieve
'long-term, high-volume orders for the lowest possible prices',
Walmart had, from the onset, invested heavily in technology.
RetailLink, its proprietary intranet that linked it with its

suppliers, enabled immediate and transparent information sharing between the suppliers and the company. Suppliers could monitor daily inventory and sales performance data for their SKUs at each Walmart warehouse and store. This was combined with a supply chain initiative called Vendor Managed Inventory (VMI), whereby manufacturers were responsible for managing their merchandise in the retailer's warehouses (called distribution centres).

This system eliminated the need for a large manufacturer salesforce or manufacturer reps calling on individual stores and reduced administrative work related to order taking and processing. The cost savings were estimated at 3–4 per cent of sales. In addition, at the manufacturer level, it did away with the need for additional inventory to support Walmart's sales while bringing production efficiencies, as suppliers could produce in response to continuous sales data from Walmart rather than intermittent bulk retail orders, which was the industry norm.

Walmart used technology as a backbone for its strategic partnerships with the largest suppliers. In contrast to the prevailing practice of using information technology systems to *audit* what happened in one's business operations, Walmart pioneered the use of information technology systems to *manage* the business operations. Because of the amount of data created and the need to analyse it for insights, the joke in the US in the 1990s was that with a physics PhD, one could work for either NASA or Walmart! Walmart had the second largest information system in the US after the Pentagon.

Its distribution network in the US, one of the largest in the world, comprised 157 distribution centres. Furthermore, Walmart's adoption of cross-docking—the direct transfer of products from inbound trucks to outbound trucks—eliminated the need for storage at distribution centres and thus helped keep the inventory and transportation costs down while also considerably reducing the delivery time. Consequently, Walmart managed to achieve almost 100 per cent order fulfilment with the lowest distribution costs in the industry. Its inbound logistics costs were 3.7 per cent compared to 4.8 per cent for the industry. Much of Walmart's competitive advantage lay in its supply chain.

Walmart's power to redefine manufacturer-retailer relationships led to a complete mindset shift among the manufacturers, especially among powerful branded players like P&G, Coca-Cola and Sony, who until then had pushed around their vulnerable retailers. By the 1990s, almost every large brand had a dedicated Walmart team with a physical office in Bentonville, Arkansas, to service the account. Manufacturers were forced to confront their brand portfolios and SKUs to assess which brands and SKUs created value for the retailer. As a result, as documented in my 2003 *Harvard Business Review* article 'Kill a Brand, Keep a Customer', almost all major companies, like Akzo-Nobel, Electrolux, Nestlé, Sara Lee and Unilever, were forced to embark on large brand and SKU rationalization programmes.[4] Many brands and SKUs that did not create triple value—for brand owner, retailer and consumer—had to be axed.

Unlike other retailers, Walmart understood that bargaining with suppliers would result in better prices until it became the world's largest retailer. After that, further bargaining had limited effect, as Walmart was already getting the best price from all its suppliers. Obtaining further reductions in the costs of goods sold required Walmart to work closely with suppliers and find ways to reduce the suppliers' costs as well as the costs of doing business with each other.

Despite their buying power, Walmart's practices were truly win-win vis-à-vis their suppliers. A study indicated that those brand manufacturers who reported Walmart (versus some other retailer) as their largest customer were more profitable. The efficiencies that Walmart forced on their suppliers had positive spillover effects on manufacturers' general operations.

People and Culture

Walmart drove a corporate culture based on frugality, in which the need to create efficiencies in operations to minimize costs was ingrained in its employees as well as its vendors. Walmart was the largest private employer in the US. Its staff was non-unionized, with half of them working on a part-time basis. To empower the store employees, Walmart shared information about store sales, profits, inventory turns, markdowns and shrinkage with them. This, combined with the store-within-store concept, encouraged departmental employees to take responsibility for the merchandise. Walmart employees demonstrated high commitment to the company and constantly offered suggestions to improve operations and lower costs.

However, the image of working at Walmart and the calibre of its employees as portrayed in the popular press was relatively poor. Many front-line employees saw a Walmart job as a transient one between changing careers or pursuing their education. By the mid-1990s, Walmart had over half a million employees in the US and the employee count was increasing by 20 per cent annually. Normally, attrition rates for the retail industry range from 20 to 100 per cent annually. Assuming even 40 per cent attrition meant that Walmart had to recruit at least 2,00,000 employees annually. My own estimate would be that it was hiring at the rate of at least 1000 employees daily. Clearly, Walmart could not be selective in hiring and engaging in any substantial training or onboarding of new recruits. The IT system was fundamental to running the business and supporting the employees with reports. It rapidly noted and communicated important variances. For example, higher labour costs in any department, relative to last year or other departments, would trigger remedial action by the departmental head to reduce staffing hours in the department.

Yet, what is invisible to naive observers is the opportunity that a fast-growth company offers to its employees. Most front-line retail employees tend not to be highly motivated, irrespective of the company. However, for the small percentage that was motivated, Walmart, with 200 new stores being opened each year and the promote-from-within approach, was a growth engine. Two hundred new stores annually, many operating twenty-four hours a day, with thirty-six departments within a store, meant that Walmart needed to add at least 200 store managers, over 1500 assistant store managers, over 7000 department heads and over 20,000 assistant department heads each year. An employee showing any ability or motivation saw rapid career advancement. The result was a combination of apathetic and highly motivated employees, where the latter, working smart and hard to continuously improve the low-cost value proposition, defined the culture at Walmart.

A Unique Business Model

Walmart's relentless focus on process improvement and costs led to dramatic growth over the 1980s, achieving dominance over the US retail segment by the early 1990s (refer to Table 2.2 for Walmart's performance over 1982–1991). In 1992, when Sam Walton passed away, Walmart recorded net sales of $44 billion, employed 3,71,000 employees across 1928 stores and clubs, was present in more than forty-five states across the US, and had gone international with its first overseas store in Mexico. Since the operations then were primarily domestic and discount stores, it allows an investigation into the business

Table 2.2. Performance of Walmart over 1982–91*

	Particulars	1982	1983	1984	1985	1986	1987	1988	1989	1990	1991
1	Sales ($ millions)	3,376	4,667	6,401	8,451	11,909	15,959	20,649	25,811	32,602	43,887
2	Cost of goods sold ($ millions)	2,458	3,418	4,722	6,361	9,053	12,282	16,057	20,070	25,500	34,786
3	Gross profit ($ millions)	918	1,249	1,679	2,090	2,856	3,677	4,592	5,741	7,102	9,101
4	Operating expenses ($ millions)	677	893	1,181	1,485	2,008	2,599	3,268	4,070	5,152	6,684
5	Operating profit ($ millions)	241	356	498	605	848	1,078	1,324	1,671	1,950	2,417
6	Net profit ($ millions)	124	196	271	327	450	628	837	1,076	1,291	1,608
7	Number of stores	551	645	756	882	1,029	1,198	1,364	1,525	1,721	1,928
8	Retail space (millions square feet)	27.70	34.35	41.85	51.20	63.27	77.80	90.60	106.00	122.00	136.70
9	Gross profit as % of sales	27.2%	26.8%	26.2%	24.7%	24.0%	23.0%	22.2%	22.2%	21.8%	20.7%
10	Operating expenses as % of sales	20.1%	19.1%	18.5%	17.6%	16.9%	16.3%	15.8%	15.8%	15.8%	15.2%
11	Operating profit as % of sales	7.1%	7.6%	7.8%	7.2%	7.1%	6.8%	6.4%	6.5%	6.0%	5.5%
12	Net profit as % of sales	3.7%	4.2%	4.2%	3.9%	3.8%	3.9%	4.1%	4.2%	4.0%	3.7%
13	Sales $ per square foot	122	136	153	165	188	205	228	244	267	321
14	Gross profit $ per square foot	33.1	36.4	40.1	40.8	45.1	47.3	50.7	54.2	58.2	66.6
15	Operating expenses $ per square foot	24.4	26.0	28.2	29.0	31.7	33.4	36.1	38.4	42.2	48.9
16	Operating profit $ per square foot	8.7	10.4	11.9	11.8	13.4	13.9	14.6	15.8	16.0	17.7
17	Net profit $ per square foot	4.5	5.7	6.5	6.4	7.1	8.1	9.2	10.2	10.6	11.8

model that Walmart pursued to achieve dominance without the numbers getting harder to interpret due to country and store format mix changes in the later years. Table 2.2 demonstrates the unique business model and the financial strategy underlying Walmart's value proposition.

To understand Walmart's disruptive business model, let us examine in greater depth the different dimensions of financial and store performance in Table 2.2:

- The numbers that are reported in the annual reports appear in the first eight rows of the table. Any observer would not fail to be impressed by the consistent growth delivered. Top-line revenues grew from $3 billion to $44 billion (row 1), or thirteen times, in ten years! The number of stores almost quadrupled (551 to 1928, row 7) while the retail space increased five times (27.7 to 136.7 million square feet, row 8), demonstrating increasing sales per store and the move to larger stores.

- The bottom line in terms of net income as a percentage of sales bounced around a bit. But over the ten years, it stayed within a narrow band (3.7 per cent to 4.2 per cent) and returned to 3.7 per cent in 1991, exactly where it started in 1982 (row 12). Clearly, the rapid sales expansion had not come at the cost of net margins.

- A traditional finance-oriented view would be concerned that the sales expansion had not resulted in increasing margins (rows 9, 11 and 12). In fact, gross margin as a percentage of sales shows a steady decline from 27.2 per cent to 20.7 per cent. Note that for a retailer, gross margin is what they add on top of the cost of goods, which is paid to the suppliers (gross margin percentage + costs of goods sold percentage = 100) to obtain the final selling prices. As a retailer becomes larger, the conventional thinking is that gross margins will expand because the retailer is able to negotiate better prices with its suppliers on account of larger orders. Here, we observe that thirteen times sales growth over a decade has resulted in the cost of goods sold as a percentage of sales increasing from 72.8 per cent to 79.3 per cent (or gross margins to mirror the decrease). This is the counter-intuitive strategic business model choice Walmart made. Unlike businesses that attempt to increase gross margin percentage over time, Walmart understood, as a retailer, that this implied increasing prices for consumers. Assuming all large retailers are paying identical prices to suppliers, adding a lower gross margin increases Walmart's competitive advantage vis-a-vis its competitors. Its strategic objective during these growth years was 'to reduce gross margins every year'! Not only was this consistent with their mission 'to lower the cost of living for the world' but also what made them so disruptive a business model and a competition killer.

- Over time, consumers rewarded Walmart for its lower prices. Reinforced by the banners in the stores blaring 'Falling Prices' and an advertising campaign with the tagline 'Always low prices, Always', shoppers were able to 'see' the price declines. This helped attract greater numbers of shoppers to Walmart. Furthermore, Walmart consumers also devoted a larger share of their wallets to the retailer. As a result, Walmart increased sales per square foot from $122 to $321 over the decade (row 13). Sales per square foot is an extremely important number in retailing because it is a proxy for how well the retailer is sweating the fixed assets (investment in stores/furnishings) and the current assets (as retail space is a good proxy for the inventory).

- More importantly, the increasing sales per square foot compensated for the decline in margins. In other words, even though the gross profit and operating profit as a percentage of sales were declining (27.2 per cent to 20.7 per cent and 7.1 per cent to 5.5 per cent, respectively, rows 9 and 11), the gross profits dollars ($33.1 to $66.6, row 14) and operating profits dollars ($8.7 to $17.7, row 16) generated per square foot kept climbing. At the end of the day, it is the absolute dollars that one banks, not the percentages—something that Walmart understood well.

- Increasing sales also helped them obtain economies of scale on operating expenses. Much of the decline in the gross profit as a percentage of sales (27.2 per cent to 20.7 per cent, row 9) was compensated by lowering operating expenses as a percentage of sales (20.1 per cent to 15.2 per cent, row 10). Simply looking at operating expenses as a percentage of sales may lead an observer to assume that Walmart was cutting costs. But this is where the beauty of increasing sales per square foot makes a dramatic difference. The operating expenses in dollar terms per square foot more than doubled from $24 to $49 per square foot (row 15). What do a retailer's operating expenses comprise? Half of them are labour costs. Since you buy labour with absolute dollars, the increasing expenses in dollar terms (accounting for some wage inflation) implies that Walmart is increasing service intensity. And voila, that's how Walmart has become the largest company in the world—reduce prices every year and increase service every year to make the value proposition to the customer more attractive and deepen its competitive differentiation.

To reveal the singularity of the Walmart mindset behind its strategy, consider the situation I observed as a consultant when a private equity firm acquired a famous loss-making retailer in the 1990s. A turnaround strategy was immediately implemented, which entailed increasing gross margins, reducing operating expenses and expecting that sales per square foot would increase. While the numbers all looked good on the Excel spreadsheet as it would lead to profitability, they forgot the logic of retailing. When you sell identical or, rather, similar products, as retailers do, increasing gross margins implies higher prices for shoppers, while decreasing operating expenses forces lower customer service. This will lead to lower, not higher, sales per square foot as consumers respond, as should be expected, negatively. Well, it took them less than a year to declare bankruptcy. Part of Walmart's people strategy was to eschew hiring MBAs from leading business schools who would come encumbered with these types of financial mental models.

Facing the Online Challenge

The 1990s ended with the birth of Amazon and the rise of online retailing. With limited success in e-commerce from 2000 to 2014, Walmart recognized the need to develop the essential e-capabilities it lacked. Through the years, Walmart introduced a variety of online grocery services, such as Walmart Pickup, which allowed customers to order online and pick up their orders at one of its stores, or Pickup Today, which allowed customers to pick up their online orders at a store within four hours for free.

To implement in-store pickup, 18,000 employees became 'personal shoppers' and had to undergo a three-week training programme in order to pick the best produce and meats. As specialists, they were paid more than the entry-level workers. Walmart also installed pickup towers near the entrance of many of its stores, which served as vending machines for non-grocery online orders. These 16-foot tall and 8-foot wide towers allowed customers to scan the barcode on the online order receipt (or enter the order number) and collect their parcel in less than 45 seconds. By 2019, Walmart had these towers available across 1500 stores.[5]

For those customers who preferred home delivery, Walmart rolled out free shipping in two days for orders larger than $35, without any membership fees (unlike Amazon Prime). To address the 'last mile connectivity' issue (considered to be the most expensive part of the fulfilment process) in a cost-effective manner, the retailer enlisted its store employees to deliver online orders on their way home from work for extra pay.

The acquisitions of private brands, such as Hayneedle in 2016, Moosejaw (outdoor apparel), ShoeBuy (Zappos-style shoe retailer), Modcloth (indie and vintage clothing) and Bonobos (menswear) in 2017, helped Walmart expand its range of online apparel and accessories merchandise to include fashion, a category in which the retailer had struggled to make its mark in the past.

In September 2017, Walmart acquired New York-based Parcel, a technology-based, 24/7 operation that delivered packages the same day, overnight and in scheduled two-hour windows. Leveraging Parcel's expertise, Walmart planned to deliver both general merchandise as well as fresh and frozen groceries to customers in New York City. In addition, to address one of the key consumer concerns associated with online grocery shopping, Walmart provided a 100 per cent money-back guarantee if the quality and freshness of the fruits and vegetables were found unsatisfactory.

In 2020, it offered Walmart+, a membership-based programme, to US consumers for a streamlined omnichannel shopping experience, which included unlimited free shipping on eligible items with no minimum order requirement, unlimited delivery from stores, fuel discounts and a mobile scan-and-go option. To the online marketplace sellers, the retailer offered in-house advertising services via Walmart Connect, and supply chain and fulfilment capabilities via Walmart Fulfilment Services.

Walmart's mobile shopping platform was instrumental in creating an omnichannel experience at its physical stores. Inside the store, the Walmart mobile app once turned on, slipped into the 'store assistant' mode, providing shoppers access to up-to-date information about the products, where they were stocked in the store, how much their shopping carts would cost when they checked out and an automated checkout process. The scan-and-go feature allowed shoppers to completely bypass the checkout lanes in-store. They could simply scan the barcodes of their selected items on the mobile app, bag them and pay directly through the app. Besides, customers buying pharmacy products or availing money services could just order prescription refills or fill out the necessary paperwork from their phone after having entered their personal information in the app. The app enabled customers to track the order status, view pricing and manage pick-up details. Moreover, the express lanes in the stores for pickup made the process even faster.

Walmart also launched a simplified return process through its mobile express returns service, whereby customers initiated the process of return on the app by selecting the online transaction and finishing it at the physical store, where they returned the item using the express lanes. The refunds were credited to the customer's account soon afterwards. The retailer also introduced personalized voice shopping (in partnership with Google) to offer hundreds of thousands of items that could be purchased by customers by simply speaking into the mobile app or on the Google Express website.

Walmart's concerted efforts towards building an omnichannel presence, accelerated by the outbreak of COVID-19, led it to achieve a high growth rate in its e-commerce sales. In 2021, it had over 8000 pickup and 6000 delivery locations globally, its website offered more than 170 million SKUs, attracting 120 million monthly visitors, and its marketplace comprised over 1,00,000 online sellers.[6,7] In addition, the company went into an alliance with e-commerce platform Shopify, enabling one million-plus merchants of Shopify to directly access Walmart's online marketplace.[8]

Walmart's efforts to master e-commerce and compete effectively against Amazon with an omnichannel proposition have resulted in 13 per cent of its revenues in 2022 being contributed by online sales. Yet, this has come at a cost. Online sales are not as profitable, and the investment needed for the delivery infrastructure is considerable. Subsequent chapters will confront these challenges of online profitability in greater detail. Here, taking a helicopter view, revisiting Table 2.1 indicates Walmart's operating income, net income and return on assets peaked in 2012. A decade later, as e-commerce operations have become an increasingly substantial part of Walmart, despite the overall firm revenues growing by 30 per cent, operating income (from $27.8 to $20.4 billion), net income (from $17.8 to $11.3 billion), and return on assets (from 9 per cent to 4.6 per cent) have declined dramatically. Without insider information, it is hard to accurately assess the earnings-dilutive effect of e-commerce on Walmart. However, as the rest of the book will demonstrate, online retailing is not a profitable business for the low-value products that Walmart or, for that matter, even Amazon, peddles.

With its investments and adoption of e-commerce, Walmart's omnichannel business model is hurtling towards Amazon. But this clash is increasingly being fought on Amazon's terms and capabilities. Amazon has investor patience, AWS and advertising to help it survive the online retailing losses and demonstrate an increasing overall profitability. In contrast, Walmart is being punished by the markets for the crushed margins that are the result of following the received market wisdom that they should be pushing online sales.

As an alternative view to considering Walmart a dinosaur in the digital world, let us reflect on Walmart's recent resurgence of physical store revenues. Walmart grew sales by 6.7 per cent, or $43.5 billion, in the year ending 31 January 2023. Just to put this growth number in context, annual revenues of Fortune 500 companies, ranked between 235 and 245 of the world's largest companies (e.g., Canon, FedEx, Mitsubishi Electric, Schlumberger), are about $43 billion. In other words, while its growth rate may pale in comparison to Amazon's, Walmart last year added revenues equivalent to the size of a Fortune Global 250 company, and this was all internally generated rather than acquisition-based growth.

Clearly, Walmart has limited choice vis-a-vis its clash with Amazon. It must continue pursuing the current omnichannel strategy as customers demand it. This requires Walmart to accept that the 13 per cent of total Walmart overall revenues coming from online sales will continue to increase while being earnings-dilutive. As will be articulated in the forthcoming chapters, like Amazon, Walmart must accelerate the monetization of its large audience by pushing for greater marketplace (third-party sales) and advertising income. Since both marketplace and advertising are highly profitable, if these grow faster than physical store sales, then Walmart's earnings profile should reverse its downward trajectory. And if it does, who knows, perhaps then Wall Street will reappreciate Walmart.

Chapter Takeaways

- Prior to the rise of e-commerce in 2000, Walmart was the disruptive retail business model. Its business practices were seen as 'best practices' by companies worldwide.

- Walmart was a pioneer in the adoption of information technology to 'manage' the business, in contrast to the then prevailing practice of using IT to 'audit' the business.
- Walmart's integrated marketing strategy rested on the 4Ps, reinforcing the interactive effects of each P on the other three Ps.
- Its value proposition of lowest prices was supported through advertising, money-back guarantees, the most efficient supply chain and a counter-intuitive financial strategy.
- The counter-intuitive financial model of reducing gross margins while growing sales per square foot underlays the value proposition of lowering prices and increasing service intensity. The increase in sales per square foot more than compensated for the lowering of gross margin in percentage terms to increase profit per square foot in dollars annually.
- The rapid increase in overall revenues and the private label programme resulted in Walmart growing larger than its more famous brand suppliers. This forced suppliers to change their view of retailers. Rather than push retailers around, suppliers had to invest in building win-win relationships through large brand and SKU portfolio rationalization initiatives.
- Since 2000, Walmart has invested considerable resources in building an e-commerce business to occupy the second position after Amazon in US online sales.
- Online retailing for Walmart has been earnings-dilutive as these sales are not as profitable as shoppers coming to the store.

3

Amazon: The E-Commerce Pioneer

In a time not so long ago, in the sprawling digital realm of Commerceville, a curious and ambitious individual named Jeff embarked on a journey that would redefine the very essence of retail.

Jeff, a visionary dreamer, observed the limitations of traditional brick-and-mortar stores. Long lines, limited selections and the hassle of travelling to various shops left customers wanting more. Inspired by the potential of the Internet, Jeff set out to create a place where people could find anything they desired, right at their fingertips.

With unwavering determination, Jeff started Amazon, an online bookstore. The year was 1994 and e-commerce was relatively uncharted territory. Little did the world know that Amazon's humble beginnings as a bookstore would soon evolve into something far greater.

Jeff's commitment to customer satisfaction was unwavering. He understood that people valued convenience and swift deliveries. He introduced a new concept, 'Amazon Prime', offering subscribers lightning-fast shipping and exclusive perks. This transformed the way people thought about online shopping, setting new expectations for speed and reliability.

As Amazon's digital shelves expanded to include items beyond books, its algorithms learnt from every click and purchase. These insights became the foundation for Amazon's personalized recommendations, making shopping feel like a personalized journey rather than a transaction. Soon, Amazon's virtual marketplace opened its doors to other sellers, democratizing retail and providing small businesses with a platform to reach a global audience. This shift turned Amazon into not just a store, but a vibrant ecosystem connecting buyers and sellers worldwide.

As technology advanced, so did Amazon's innovations. The introduction of the Kindle e-reader ignited a digital reading revolution, while Alexa, the AI-powered assistant, brought the future directly into people's homes. And then came Amazon Web Services (AWS), a groundbreaking cloud computing service that not only transformed businesses but also laid the foundation for Amazon's own scale and growth.

But Jeff's vision extended beyond the digital realm. In a surprising move, Amazon acquired Whole Foods Market, bridging the gap between online and physical retail. The blend of e-commerce expertise and the tactile experience of a grocery store showcased a new frontier in retail possibilities.

As the years went by, Amazon's impact became undeniable. It had altered the way people shopped, inspired businesses to embrace digital transformation and even shifted the landscape of job markets. The story of Amazon wasn't just that of a company; it was a testament to the power of audacious dreams and a relentless pursuit of excellence.

The Rise of Amazon

On 5 July 2019, Amazon completed twenty-five years of existence. The previous month, June 2019, with a brand value of $113 billion, Amazon had overtaken Apple and Google to become the world's most valuable brand. Going from strength to strength, on 4 February 2020, Amazon's market capitalization closed at above a trillion dollars for the first time! In the process, its founder, Jeff Bezos, became the world's richest person, with a personal fortune estimated at easily over $100 billion. A remarkable company, with its visionary founder, had transformed the retailing world with its pioneering online foray.

Launched in 1994 by Bezos as a company that sold books online, Amazon expanded extensively over the years to retail more than thirty-six product categories, which included electronics, music, toys, groceries, apparel, footwear and appliances. Between 1994 and 2022, e-commerce and Amazon shared a symbiotic relationship, with growth in one fuelling the other. As the number of people using the Internet in the US multiplied from 40 million in 1997 to over 300 million in 2022,[1] and online sales grew by more than 300 times (from $2.4 billion to over a trillion dollars), Amazon's sales and stock prices too grew in equal measure (refer to Table 3.1 for Amazon's performance over 2002–22).[2] In the process, Amazon established itself as the second largest company in the world in terms of revenues, only behind Walmart. Of Amazon's $514 billion 2022 revenues, online stores, Marketplace, AWS, other (mostly advertising), Prime subscriptions and physical stores accounted for 220, 118, 80, 42, 35 and 19 billion dollars, respectively.

Marketplace

Initially, Amazon was conceptualized as an online retailer that purchased goods from suppliers, held them in inventory and shipped them to customers in response to orders. This contrasted with Alibaba or eBay, which were true marketplaces, simply connecting suppliers with customers and collecting

Table 3.1. Amazon Financial Performance

In USD million except for the calculated values/ratios	2002	2007	2012	2017	2022
Operating Results					
Net sales	3,993	14,835	61,093	1,77,866	5,13,983
Total operating expenses	3,868	14,180	60,417	1,73,760	5,01,735
Operating income (Loss)	64	655	676	4,106	12,248
Operating expenses break-up					
Cost of sales (a)	2,490	11,482	45,971	1,11,934	2,88,831
Fulfilment (b)	392	1,292	6,419	25,249	84,299
Marketing	125	344	2,408	10,069	42,238
Technology and content (c)	216	818	4,564	22,620	73,213
General and administrative	79	235	896	3,674	11,891
Others	116	9	159	214	1,263
Total	3,868	14,180	60,417	1,73,760	5,01,735

In USD million except for the calculated values/ratios	2002	2007	2012	2017	2022
	Financial Position				
Inventory	202	1,200	6,031	16,047	53,888
Total assets	1,990	6,485	32,555	1,31,310	4,62,675
Return on assets	(7.5%)	7.3%	(0.1%)	2.3%	(0.6%)
Diluted earnings per share	(0.39)	1.12	(0.09)	6.15	(0.27)
Total stockholders' equity (deficit)	(1,353)	1,197	8,192	27,709	1,46,043
Return on equity	(11.0%)	39.7%	(0.5%)	11.0%	(1.9%)
Free cash flow	135	1,181	395	8,376	(11,569)
Shipping costs (included in cost of sales)	404	1,174	5,134	21,700	83,500
No. of Employees (worldwide)	7,500	17,000	88,400	560,000	1,600,000

Financial year end on 31 December

a: Includes both inbound and outbound shipping costs

b: Comprises the operating and staffing cost of fulfilment centres, customer service centres and physical stores, and payment processing costs

c: Includes the cost of technical staff, technical equipment and infrastructure required to support AWS

Source: Amazon.com Inc. Annual Reports

commissions on the transactions. Marketplaces were relatively asset-light, not requiring inventory management, with greater profitability as they did not engage in the heavy lifting associated with Amazon's online sales (supply chain management, inventory and fulfilment). When marketplace suppliers used the fulfilment services of the platform, the suppliers had to pay the marketplaces for them, above and beyond the sales commission.

In 2000, Amazon launched its 'Marketplace', allowing third-party sellers on the platform. By 2020, it had more than 1.9 million active sellers worldwide (including about 5,00,000 US-based small and medium businesses), who made up 60 per cent of Amazon's gross merchandise value.[3] From 5.5 million SKUs in 2000, the company expanded to 350 million by 2020. In 2022, commissions charged to third parties for their sales on the Amazon platform, as well as services charged to these vendors, accounted for $117 billion of Amazon's revenue. The gross merchandise value (GMV) of third-party sellers on Amazon was estimated at over $600 billion, in contrast to Amazon's own online retail sales of $220 billion. Note that only approximately 15 per cent of the commission that Amazon charges Marketplace vendors, plus any paid services provided, are booked as Amazon revenues from Marketplace (i.e., $117 billion on $600 billion of GMV).

Marketplace allowed Amazon to offer a much larger assortment without bearing the associated inventory costs. Amazon's online sales concentrated on stocking the high-demand, high-velocity items, letting Marketplace sellers offer the long-tail items (those items that are infrequently purchased and with low demand). The resulting larger assortment made Amazon a default option for customers to turn to when shopping online as no matter what a customer needed, it was likely to be available on Amazon. The increasing integration on the website of Amazon's own offerings and the marketplace offerings made the entire process seamless for customers. This made Prime membership a more compelling proposition. Besides, Marketplace sales were more profitable for Amazon relative to sales of those products that it had in its own inventory and for which Amazon had to bear the entire fulfilment costs.

Amazon Web Services

Despite criticism from markets that it would dilute Amazon's focus on its core online retail business, AWS, an on-demand cloud computing platform for individuals, companies and governments, continued to gather momentum from its initial hesitant launch in the early 2000s. Instead of limiting investment in cloud infrastructure to the extent that would be needed to run their own online retail business, and therefore be a cost, Amazon made an inspired choice to offer it as a service to everyone.

This had several benefits. To make it a business, Amazon had to be extremely efficient and lead cloud computing rather than simply being a customer reliant on third-party providers. Second, by having external customers, it brought scale to the cloud operations, lowering costs both for itself and for its cloud-computing customers. Third, it has been a financially lucrative business segment for Amazon. In 2022, it was Amazon's most profitable business segment, generating an operating income of $22.8 billion on revenues of $80.1 billion. In fact, until 2016, the operating income from the AWS segment was greater than Amazon's overall operating income, implying the non-AWS part of the firm was losing money.

The first mover advantage of Amazon into cloud computing has made AWS a dominant player in what is now a more than $200 billion industry annually. While competition has increased, Amazon is still the market leader with an estimated 34 per cent market share, followed by Microsoft Azure at 21 per cent and Google Cloud at 11 per cent. Although these three leaders account for more than two-thirds of the industry, major technology giants such as IBM, Oracle and Salesforce are increasingly prioritizing cloud computing, while Alibaba and Tencent lead in the Chinese market. Besides profitability, cloud computing also has the advantage of being a stable subscription business as customers generally renew and ramp up their consumption. This brings stability in sales and earnings for Amazon.

Amazon Prime

Recognizing that the real impediment to greater adoption of the online model was the cost of delivery and the delivery time, in 2005, Amazon Prime was launched. For an annual subscription of $79 in the US, members could have unlimited free two-day delivery on a large number of items.[4] Over time, Amazon added a host of other benefits to sweeten the pot, beginning with free access to a certain number of books, Prime Video (movies, soaps and music), unlimited cloud photo storage space and the annual Prime Day sales event.

Inspired by the success of Alibaba's Singles Day (11/11) event in China, in July 2015, Amazon launched Prime Day, an exclusive annual sale event for Amazon Prime members, offering big discounts on select products ranging from electronics to clothing and homeware. Each year in July, Amazon offers the event to more countries and across a wider range of products, while Prime members steadily increase their spending. In 2023, the event was available in more than twenty countries, with Prime Day sales of $13 billion. The retailer sold 375 million items worldwide. In the three-week lead-up to Prime Day, customers had purchased more than 100 million items from small businesses, generating $3 billion in sales. Third-party sales on Prime Day were two to four times of sales on a regular shopping day.

The Prime Day event held in the summer, typically a slower period for retailers, not only generates sales but also acts as a big advertisement, serving to attract new Prime subscribers. Furthermore, enrolling non-Prime customers in the summer allows the retailer to capture their back-to-school, Labour Day and end-of-the-year holidays/festival shopping. Amazon has now added 'Prime Big Deals Day' in October, hoping to prepone consumer Christmas shopping.

To boost its share specifically in the grocery and apparel categories, Amazon introduced many Prime services that significantly enhanced customer value. Its 'Prime Now' service provided members with free two-hour delivery on a large selection of grocery items. In addition, to facilitate trials during online clothes shopping, in 2017 it launched 'Prime Wardrobe', which allowed shoppers to try on clothes at home before paying. Members could order multiple items of clothing (up to eight items), keep whatever they wanted and send the rest back. They were charged only for the items that were kept. Shipping was free both ways.

Amazon Prime membership globally grew from 4 million in 2011 to 65 million in 2016, and in 2022, the retailer boasted of having over 200 million subscribers, generating $35 billion in subscription fees. In 2021, Prime shoppers in the US received more than 6 billion free deliveries.[5] Amazon raised Prime's annual subscription price from $119 to $139, the first increase since 2018 and as a result, growth in membership has slowed in the US. However, annual fees in other countries are substantially lower, equivalent to $115 in the UK, $72 in Canada and less than $20 in India.

The impact of Amazon Prime on consumer behaviour has been substantial. Prime members see Amazon as the first place to turn to when they need to buy any item. With no delivery cost to the shopper, no need to combine orders to save on shipping costs and delivery usually on the next day since 2019, Amazon has become the default shopping option for households with Prime membership. Studies indicate that 91 per cent of Prime members consider only Amazon for their online purchases. On average, Amazon Prime customers spend over $3000 per year on the e-commerce site, almost twice as much spent by non-members.[6] Moreover, 98 per cent of those who had been Prime members for two years renewed their membership.[7]

Private Label Brands

In 2009, Amazon began its private label programme by introducing batteries under its brand AmazonBasics, targeting cost-conscious consumers. With AmazonBasics quickly grabbing a one-third share of the market, the company not only expanded its private label programme to over fourteen categories, from electronics to home necessities but also launched multiple in-house brands across various product categories to help boost thin retail margins. With increased focus on apparel, Amazon launched several labels over the years that spanned women's, men's, children's and infants' clothing, and catered to a wide spectrum, from basics (e.g., Amazon Essentials) to those with more fashion content (e.g., Lark & Ro, Goodthreads and Core10). The retailer also had exclusive lines like Spotted Zebra for kids' clothing and Buttoned Down for men's business wear. By 2023, Amazon's portfolio of private labels included around 120 brands.

Access to data on consumers' product and price preferences helped Amazon develop its private label brands accordingly. In some cases, by simply mimicking the bestselling products in the category and selling at a lower price. Insight into what consumers were searching for helped it understand gaps in the market and in its own assortment. For example, when Ralph Lauren was unwilling to list its polo shirts on the Amazon site, customers searching for them were instead presented polo shirts from Amazon Essentials (its affordable clothing line for various occasions) in twelve different colours at $12 each.

Of course, as described in my *Private Label Strategy* book, traditional retailers, including Walmart, had been pursuing this strategy forever.[8] However, given its online operating environment, Amazon had certain advantages relative to traditional brick-and-mortar retailers with respect to the development and marketing of private labels. In developing private labels, Amazon could mine customer reviews to understand the pain points of the customers, such as a shirt fading after five washes. Beyond information on what was bought and what was returned by customers, which traditional retailers also have access to, Amazon knows which search terms are popular, what people are clicking on before deciding what to finally buy and how much time a shopper spends considering the different alternatives. When it comes to marketing, while traditional retailers have always given preferential shelf position to their private labels relative to the manufacturer brands, there are limits to what a physical store retailer can do. In contrast, if Amazon so desires, it can feature its private labels on the top of the results to a search query by a shopper, while placing the manufacturer or Marketplace products on, say, page 10! Retailers, including Amazon, favour private labels relative to third-party supplier brands because of the higher margins their own labels generate.

As Amazon became larger in absolute size and more dominant in e-commerce, its private label programme attracted antitrust scrutiny from regulators. In 2020, the US Congress held hearings on whether Amazon was unfairly using its marketplace data of third-party sales to benefit Amazon private labels. The European Commission charged Amazon with using its power and data to gain an unfair advantage over marketplace merchants. In response to these pressures, Amazon agreed to limit its use of marketplace seller data. Bezos, during the congressional hearings, remarked, 'We have a policy against using seller specific data to aid our private-label business . . . But I can't guarantee you that policy has never been violated.'[9]

Advertising

Over the years, consumers in the US increasingly used Amazon to search for products (refer to Figure 3.1 for more details). By 2016, Amazon had overtaken Google as the site on which Internet users typically began product searches.[10] However, Bezos was a late convert to the potential of advertising as a source of revenue for Amazon. Advertising revenues for Amazon, while not separately disclosed in its financial statements (part of 'other') until 2022, were growing rapidly. In 2019, it integrated Amazon Media Group, Amazon Marketing Services and the Amazon Advertising Platform into one category as Amazon Advertising.

In 2022, for the first time, Amazon revealed its revenues from advertising for FY 2021 as over $31 billion, up 32 per cent from the previous year, but did not divulge its profitability. The advertising revenues increased another 21 per cent in 2022 to reach $37.7 billion. Amazon is now a serious player in the online advertising industry against well-established competitors such as Meta and Google, and the trio accounts for over half of the global online ad spending. A survey of digital advertising revenue share worldwide reveals that Amazon now holds 7.3 per cent of the overall online ad market. Amazon is trailing Google's 28.8 per cent share as well as Meta-owned Facebook

Figure 3.1. Platforms Searched for Online Shopping

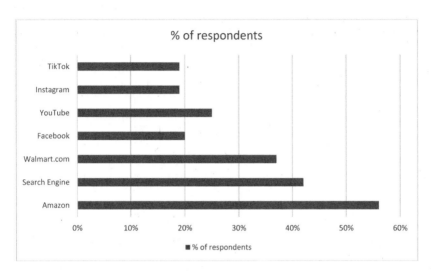

Adapted from: Jungle Scout, Consumer Trends Report Q1 2023

and Instagram, which, respectively, have 11.4 per cent and 9.1 per cent of the digital ad market.[11] Unlike Google and Meta, which experienced falling revenues in 2022, Amazon advertising is still growing rapidly.

The algorithms utilized by these three companies to optimize the placement of advertisements rely on different variables based on their respective user data. Given the ubiquity of the Android operating system on mobile phones, Google's advertising algorithm uses user location data and context (previous searches) to present the search results and the most relevant advertising. For example, a search for 'Egypt' would show travel-related content for a moderate, Muslim brotherhood for a conservative, and 2011 uprising for the liberal-leaning user. Based on past searches, Google can assess the political leanings of the person searching. Similarly, a search for coffee is optimized by showing cafes located in physical proximity to the user. In contrast, Facebook relies more on the demographic data of users (called 'look-alikes' at Facebook) and their self-expressed interests to present the most relevant advertising.

Amazon, on the other hand, uses past purchase history to present the relevant assortment of products and advertising. Since past purchases are the best predictor of future purchases, Amazon's algorithm has a built-in advantage (in terms of getting the user to click and purchase) with respect to advertising. Furthermore, the ease of purchasing using one click on Amazon results in greater conversion of the clicks into purchases relative to Google or Meta. It is reasonable to assume that advertising is more profitable (from a margin perspective) for Amazon than for its competitors Google and Meta. Amazon is simply repurposing its existing past sales information, while Google and Meta need to continuously invest to maintain search and social capabilities to generate the required customer data to sell advertising.

Technology and AI Initiatives

In 2015, Amazon launched the first-generation Amazon Echo, a smart speaker that responds to voice commands. The features of the fourth-gen model launched in 2020 include voice interaction, providing weather, traffic and other real-time information, playing music and audiobooks, making to-do lists, setting alarms, streaming podcasts and controlling other smart devices by acting as a home automation hub.

In 2012, Amazon started using robotics in its facilities to help move carts and packages. Sparrow, its latest warehouse robot, introduced in 2022, can handle millions of items. The robot leverages computer vision and artificial intelligence to detect, select and handle individual products in Amazon's inventory.

In 2017, Amazon acquired Body Labs to gain the AI technology that created 3D models for shoppers to try clothes online and recommend tailoring. With its use, the retailer aims to create a realistic 3D model of an individual's body from just an image, including specific individual characteristics, and add motion to the models in order to see how certain fabrics move and fit. To this end, Amazon has been conducting research in the US and the UK by taking digital 3D 'scans' of volunteers.

Generative artificial intelligence is having dramatic effects on many aspects of Amazon. Since building a proprietary engine like ChatGPT would require an investment of billions of dollars, a game in which Google and Microsoft are ahead of Amazon, Amazon has taken a different tack. It will build capabilities on top of existing foundational AI models that result in giving Amazon and its AWS customers the ability to customize models for their own purposes. For example, using Amazon's Titan model, AWS customers can customize models using their own data, but the customer data will not be used to train the Titan model. This ensures that one's own customer data does not help benefit competitors.

AI is also helping Amazon with providing better search results, recommendations and personalization for its e-commerce consumers. To drive advertising revenues and be a more effective competitor to Google and Meta in this space, Amazon is using AI tools to generate photos and videos for merchants to use on the Amazon platform. In the future, product descriptions can be written and optimized for sales using AI. It will enable the development of more effective advertising campaigns for its marketplace vendors and increase conversions for Amazon of browsers to buyers. AI algorithms are also deployed to analyse large amounts of data from customer behaviour patterns, sales history and user reviews to identify potentially fraudulent activities and recommend appropriate action.

AI is fundamental to delivering future efficiencies in supply chain and fulfilment. By analysing historical sales patterns, seasonality as well as external factors such as events and weather, AI helps Amazon forecast demand more accurately. This helps Amazon optimize inventory and minimize stockouts—thus simultaneously reducing inventory holding costs and ensuring product availability. Furthermore, AI helps predict which Amazon warehouse to fulfil a consumer order from, shipping products in anticipation of customer demand to closer local delivery points and routing delivery trucks. All of this reduces fulfilment costs and increases the speed of delivery.

As an application of AI, consider the problem of damaged merchandise. Around one of 1000 items Amazon handles are damaged and should not be shipped to the customer as it will trigger an expensive refund and return process.[12] Amazon has found that relative to warehouse workers, AI is three times more likely to identify damaged merchandise during the picking and packing process. Using photos of damaged items versus perfect items, the AI engine of the imaging station has been trained to either pass an item, reject if damaged or sometimes, pass it to a manual worker for a closer look to make the final determination.

A Unique Business Model: Focus on Customers, Not Profits

From the very beginning, Amazon's key decisions and plans had been firmly and consistently driven by a focus on developing long-term market leadership through customer orientation, rather than accruing short-term profitability—a promise that is reiterated every year to its shareholders. This approach allows Amazon to continuously experiment with its business model and launch innovative services for customers. Jeff Bezos has run his company according to an unconventional set of core principles: don't worry about competitors, don't worry about making money for shareholders and don't worry about the short-term. Focus on the customers, and everything else will fall into place. This customer obsession has been implemented relentlessly to build Amazon's unique culture, manifesting itself in the following principles, policies and practices over the years:

- *Always keep the customer at the centre of the business.* Occasionally, Bezos leaves an empty chair in the conference room and considers it occupied by the most important person in the room: the customer. As he noted in his 1998 newsletter, 'I constantly remind our employees to be afraid, to wake up every morning terrified. Not of our competition, but of our customers. Our customers have made our business what it is, they are the ones with whom we have a relationship, and they are the ones to whom we owe a great obligation. And we consider them to be loyal to us—right up until the second that someone else offers them a better service.'[13]

- *Personalization* rather than segmentation is what makes marketing at Amazon so powerful. Given the unique data they have on individual customers—what they browsed, what they did not buy and what they purchased—Amazon can observe the 'no' decision of customers that a physical retailer, limited by purchase data, cannot. The continuously improving powerful recommendation engine is among Amazon's distinctive capabilities, as past purchases of a customer are the best predictor of future purchases. A physical retailer must present the same store to all incoming customers as any individual store is limited to being customized based only on the characteristics of the neighbourhood it is located in. In contrast, through collaborative filtering, Amazon's recommendation engine allows the store (landing page of the customer) to be not only different for each individual but also different for the same individual over time. As a result, Amazon does not need to work with customer segments, focusing instead on individual customers' real-time needs.

- *Relentless dissatisfaction*, because according to Bezos, 'when we're at our best, we don't wait for external pressures. We are internally driven to improve our services, adding benefits and features, before we have to. We lower prices and increase value for customers before we have to. We invent before we have to.'[14] This desire to measure oneself by one's customers runs deep in Amazon, as in Bezos's words, they are always 'beautifully, wonderfully dissatisfied'.[15] If Amazon focuses on always trying to make customers happier, it is hard to go wrong. For example, one Christmas season, Amazon delivered 99.9 per cent on time, but Bezos was unhappy that one out of 1000 customers did not get the delivery as promised.

- *Culture of metrics*, but non-financial, customer metrics. Amazon tracks 500 measurable goals, 80 per cent of which are customer-related, like out-of-stocks, speed of download and quality of recommendations. Once, Bezos wanted to develop an e-book that could be downloaded in 60 seconds as he believed it would delight the customer. The finance director asked: How much do you want to spend on it? Bezos snapped back, 'How much do we have?'

- *De-emphasize financials*. As Bezos observed, 'Senior leaders that are new to Amazon are often surprised by how little time we spend discussing actual financial results or debating projected financial outputs. To be clear, we take these financial outputs seriously, but we believe that focusing our energy on the controllable inputs to our business is the most effective way to maximize financial outputs over time . . .

We have a high bar for the experience our customers deserve and a sense of urgency to improve that experience.'[16]

- *Coddle the customers, not the employees* has always been the Amazon way. The culture is built on challenging the other person in meetings, stepping on toes and speaking up. The belief is that if you do not adopt these behaviours as an employee, you are doing the company a disservice. However, when disagreeing, Amazon employees are expected to have the data to back up their argument and to expect aggressive questioning in return. Furthermore, the disagree and commit principle requires leaders to commit fully to the decision made, even if they still disagree.

- *Experimentation and innovation* for the customer have been at the heart of Amazon's success. As observed in the 2017 letter to shareholders, 'How do you stay ahead of ever-rising customer expectations? There's no single way to do it—it's a combination of many things. But high standards (widely deployed and at all levels of detail) are certainly a big part of it. We've had some successes over the years in our quest to meet the high expectations of customers. We've also had billions of dollars' worth of failures along the way.'[17]

- *Keeping margins razor-thin*, as part of its mission to become the best place to buy just about everything. As Bezos has said, 'Your margin is my opportunity.'[18] Amazon only turned profitable in 2003, a decade after its founding. Even then, despite billions in accumulated sales, its net profits were in the millions. Only after 2015 did Amazon make a few billion dollars in profits and that also was entirely on account of AWS, rather than its core online retail businesses.

- *Prioritizing cash flows over earnings* as its financial metric. 'Why focus on cash flows? Because a share of stock is a share of a company's future cash flows, and, as a result,

cash flows, more than any other single variable, seem to
do the best job of explaining a company's stock price over
the long term.'[19] Minimizing inventory, collecting payment
from customers thirty days before paying the suppliers and
managing capital investments is the key to cash generation.

Similar to the discussion in the previous chapter on Walmart,
the above demonstrates that Amazon also has a unique business
model. What is remarkable is that despite their apparent
differences, Amazon and Walmart share many characteristics. A
customer obsession, even if Amazon has taken it to an extreme.
Cost consciousness prevails at both firms, with continuous
efforts to lower costs and work off minimal margins, though
Walmart maintains profit discipline while Amazon has taught
investors to be patient on profitability. There is a shared belief in
information technology as a critical driver of business success.
The supply chain is a critical differentiator and capability for
both firms, but their focus is different. Walmart's aim is to
reduce the costs of moving boxes of products from supplier
factories to its stores, while Amazon is targeting the costs of
moving individual packages to customers' homes. Clearly, these
are two remarkable companies, forging innovative business
models against the grain and industry conventions. Copying
them requires not just simply adopting the business model, but
also a unique financial approach to operations and a mindset
that breaks with strongly held beliefs.

Brick and Mortar Presence

Amazon invested heavily in creating an offline presence to
provide shoppers with a physical browsing experience as well as
in offering click-and-collect services. However, the experience
has not met the success it expected. The twenty-four bookstores

did not find resonance with the larger audience, generating negligible revenues for the retailer. Similarly, the eighty-seven pop-up stores/kiosks did not see enough traction, and by 2021, only seven such stores were left.[20]

The 2017 acquisition of Whole Foods allowed Amazon to broaden its physical footprint, own a reputed, high-quality private label brand (called 365) and acquire a better understanding of shoppers' grocery buying behaviour through access to rich customer data. As its first steps, Amazon slashed the prices at Whole Foods by 25–50 per cent on select products to lure customers from the competition, made Whole Foods products available on its website and included them in its Prime Now service.[21] It was now able to offer customers high-quality groceries, which included thousands of natural and organic products as well as locally sourced favourites, at low prices, delivered fresh.

According to Jeff Wilke, CEO, Amazon Worldwide Consumer, 'We're determined to make healthy and organic food affordable for everyone. Everybody should be able to eat Whole Foods Market quality—we will lower prices without compromising Whole Foods Market's long-held commitment to the highest standards . . . and continuously lower prices as we invent together.'[22] Amazon also planned to use the Whole Foods stores' parking lots to drive offline cross-selling by parking its treasure trucks there and by offering merchandise that Whole Foods shoppers might be interested in purchasing.

In January 2018, after five years of research and testing, Amazon came up with another retail invention that appeared to be the future of brick-and-mortar stores. It opened Amazon Go, a fully automated convenience store with no checkout required, in Seattle, USA. The 'just walk out' shopping experience allowed shoppers to pick up items from the shelves and simply walk out. A custom-built combination of computer vision, sensor fusion and deep learning tracked the shoppers, tallied up their bill and charged it to the customers' Amazon account. While the customers benefited by controlling the amount of time they spent at a store irrespective of how crowded it was, there were concerns about whether they would be interested in such a solution, where there was no human interaction at all. The retailer believed that while it might take a little while for people to get used to simply walking out, over time, it could become practically indispensable. As Bezos said,

> *Even when they don't yet know it, customers want something better, and your desire to delight customers will drive you to invent on their behalf. No customer ever asked Amazon to create the Prime membership programme, but it sure turns out they wanted it.*[23]

By February 2020, Amazon's physical footprint included twenty-six Amazon Go cashier-less convenience stores, two Amazon Go Grocery stores, twenty-nine Amazon four-star general merchandise stores and 502 Whole Foods stores.[24]

Amazon undisputedly rules online retailing. Yet, despite the many experiments above with various formats of physical stores, Amazon's performance on this front has been underwhelming. Running physical stores is a capability that Walmart has mastered, but is far from the distinctive capabilities of Amazon. Even Whole Foods, five years after its acquisition, has grown only 10 per cent overall (over this period, Walmart has grown more than 25 per cent). This was despite the fear of many traditional retailers at the time of the acquisition that Amazon would reinvent physical retailing. As a result, the new Amazon CEO, Andy Jassy, seems to have pulled back from the brick-and-mortar network. They are closing many of the physical stores and giving up leases. Whole Foods will probably continue to grow but at the rate of a good brick-and-mortar supermarket chain, not a paradigm-busting retailer. In terms of its clash with Walmart, Amazon appears to have realized its own sweet spot lies in dominating the fast-growing e-commerce world rather than venturing into physical retail against established competitors such as Walmart. Omnichannel is a strategic imperative for Walmart, but not so much for Amazon.

Chapter Takeaways

- Amazon's symbiotic relationship with the growth of online retailing has resulted in it becoming one of the world's most valuable brands.
- Adding Marketplace to online retailing allows Amazon to provide customers with a more complete assortment (as the long tail of products is left to marketplace vendors), increase Amazon's profitability and make Prime a more compelling proposition.
- Launched against prevailing wisdom, AWS has generated most of Amazon's profits and achieved an industry-leading position in a fast-growing business.
- Prime has removed delivery costs from customer consideration, thereby making Amazon the default for Prime customers to purchase anything via one click and have it delivered the next day.
- Amazon's private label programme is more effective in developing product propositions than traditional retailers. Via customer reviews, Amazon has unique insights into what customers searched for and did not purchase ('no' decisions) as well as the pain points.
- Amazon is now a major player in online advertising. Its algorithm for placing advertisements benefits from past customer purchase data, which is the best predictor of future

purchases. In addition, unlike its two largest competitors, Google and Meta, it does not need to invest in building the search and social capabilities for generating advertising revenues.

- Amazon's many experimental store formats as well as its Whole Foods acquisition have been underwhelming. Perhaps Amazon and Walmart are best viewed as coexisting in strategic complementarity, rather than as direct competitors. Both companies share features such as customer obsession, cost consciousness, supply chain excellence and leveraging information technology, which underlie their individual success.

- Amazon coddles customers and prioritizes cash flow while it pushes its employees hard and de-emphasizes profitability.

4

The Battle for Customers

In the charming suburban town of Harmonyville lived a woman named Elimijn, a dedicated and caring housewife. Her days were filled with taking care of her family, managing the household and pursuing her creative hobbies. Two giants, Amazon and Walmart, played unexpected and integral roles in her life's journey.

Elimijn was an avid reader and an aspiring artist. She loved exploring different genres of books and finding new sources of inspiration for her art. Amazon became her digital haven, offering an extensive collection of books, art supplies and crafting tools. With a few clicks, Elimijn could order the latest bestseller, a set of watercolour paints or even a specialized easel, all delivered right to her doorstep.

But Elimijn's affection for retail didn't end online. Walmart, with its sprawling store just a short drive away, provided a unique sensory experience. Elimijn enjoyed the tactile pleasure of wandering through its aisles, exploring a vast variety of products. She would often visit with a list in hand, making her way through the neatly organized shelves, hand-picking fresh groceries, household essentials and even some affordable fashion finds.

What set Amazon and Walmart apart in Elimijn's heart was their balance in her life. Amazon's convenience saved her time and effort, allowing her to spend more precious moments with her family and immerse herself in her hobbies. On the other hand, Walmart's physical presence gave her a chance to step out, breathe in the air and indulge in a bit of old-fashioned retail therapy.

During holidays, Amazon's quick shipping helped Elimijn avoid the holiday rush. She could order thoughtful gifts for her loved ones, wrapping them up with care and sharing the joy of giving. But the annual tradition of visiting Walmart to select the perfect Christmas tree with her family remained unchanged. The smell of pine needles, the twinkling lights and the festive atmosphere created cherished memories that couldn't be replicated online.

Elimijn's relationship with these retail giants wasn't just about transactions. It was about the roles they played in her life's narrative. Amazon's efficiency became a trusted ally in her daily routine, while Walmart's physical presence provided a sense of connection to her community. In a surprising twist, Elimijn's creative endeavours gained recognition online. Her artwork found a following on social media, and soon enough, she was approached by both Amazon and Walmart to collaborate on exclusive lines of products. Amazon showcased her art supplies and books, while Walmart featured her artwork on select merchandise.

Elimijn found herself at the crossroads of the very stores she had come to love. Her story was a reminder that these giants weren't just about commerce—they were about opportunities, experiences and connections. Through Elimijn's journey, Amazon and Walmart became not just retailers, but integral parts of her life, shaping her routines, her passions and even her dreams.

Valued Customer: Who Shops at Amazon and Walmart?

The battle between Amazon and Walmart, or more generally between online retail and physical stores, is often presented as a zero-sum game. It is believed that as online retailing becomes more popular, consumers will increasingly abandon brick-and-mortar stores. Clearly, there is some evidence supporting this as many traditional retail chains have gone bankrupt while online retailers like Amazon and Alibaba continue to deliver dramatic growth numbers. This difference in growth is also reflected, as noted earlier, in the hefty valuation that the markets place on disruptive e-commerce players relative to incumbent physical retailers.

In this chapter, we will build a more nuanced picture of this competition. Specifically, we will investigate if there are certain types of customers, particular buying situations and some product categories where the relative attractiveness of physical stores like Walmart is superior to online stores like Amazon and vice versa. In exploring this, we will restrict our focus to the US, as it is the country where online retailing began and is most evolved, while also being the largest source of revenue for both Amazon and Walmart. Furthermore, we will use my *Marketing as Strategy* book's 3Vs framework of valued customer (who to serve?), value proposition (what to offer?) and value network (how to deliver?) to investigate the differences between these two retail giants.[1] The valued customer and value proposition aspects are discussed in this chapter, while the value network will be the focus of the next two chapters.

Who is the target segment for each retailer? Market segments, as we are taught, should be mutually exclusive and collectively exhaustive. Therefore, instinctively, marketers seek to answer this question by demonstrating that the types of people, based on demographic variables such as age, sex, education, income and geographical location, who prefer Amazon are different from those who patronize Walmart for their shopping needs. However, customers in the real world, as the data will show, do not fall neatly into well-defined boxes.

When asked, people often respond that relative to Walmart, Amazon shoppers are younger, more urban and educated, with higher income levels. They also see Amazon shoppers as more technologically savvy, forgetting that ordering on the mobile phone app is not a novelty or challenging any more. While the data does feed this stereotype to some extent, the differences in these demographic variables between Amazon and Walmart shoppers are not that dramatic, and furthermore, are decreasing over time.

Research indicates that the average (mean level) income of Amazon shoppers at $84,449 is only 11 per cent higher than for those who shop at Walmart ($76,313).[2] Digging deeper, the typical (modal level) Walmart shopper is a married white woman with an undergraduate degree, between fifty-five and sixty-four years old, living in the suburbs of south-eastern USA, earning about $80,000 annually.[3] However, this segment also frequents Amazon because Amazon's typical shopper is a college-educated married woman, living in the south-east, earning more than $80,000 a year, but split across two age brackets: thirty-five to forty-four and fifty-five to sixty-four.[4] Thus, a segmentation based on demographic variables does not give an accurate picture, as consumers do not shop exclusively at either Amazon or Walmart, which I am sure also reflects the behaviour of any American reader of this book.

Keeping in mind that in the past year, 95 per cent of all US adult consumers shopped at a Walmart store, while 70 per cent shopped at Amazon, there must be a large overlap between the customers of the two retailers. Almost all Amazon customers also shop at Walmart, while about three-quarters of Walmart customers must shop at Amazon. As recently as 2017, only 42 per cent of US adults made a purchase at Amazon. Then, the demographic profile of the typical Amazon versus Walmart shopper would have been more distinct. However, as the proportion of US adults shopping at Amazon has risen to the current 70 per cent, and will continue to climb in the future, it is inevitable that almost all US shoppers will be patronizing both these mega-retailers.

In other words, it is not a question any more of 'who' shops on Amazon versus at Walmart stores. Instead, the right question is why customers sometimes prefer e-commerce sites like Amazon versus a trip to a physical store like Walmart. Customers select one channel over the other according to their needs in a particular buying situation or the specific benefits sought at the time of purchase (e.g., the ability to wait for delivery or the need to touch, feel and see items before purchase). Furthermore, the importance of these benefits for consumers differs by product category. This also explains why retailers are going omnichannel—the customer now expects to move seamlessly between online and offline shopping.

As the demographic distinction between the two retailers disappears, one must compare the value propositions offered by Amazon and Walmart to understand when consumers prefer one over the other. To accurately identify the perceived value of the two retailers, a 'needs-based' segmentation approach is more relevant than traditional demographic segmentation.

Value Proposition: What do Amazon and Walmart offer?

The core value offered by Walmart Supercenters to its customers is financial benefits through bulk shopping, also called basket economics, in which a customer buys a basket worth of goods and that leads to significant savings on the overall cost. It also has a time-saving component to the value it offers because a customer can shop for a wide range of products under one roof. On the other hand, the primary focus of Amazon is convenience or ease of shopping. Amazon offers its customers time-saving (not having to travel to the store), less hassle (one-click ordering) and the ability to buy almost anything (endless aisle). It may also contribute towards some cost savings since no travel is required.

To examine the value proposition of these two retailers, let us compare Amazon online with Walmart stores using the value curve methodology, which offers an easy-to-grasp pictorial approach.[5] Through this exercise, it will be revealed that the two retailers have distinct value propositions. Clearly, these value propositions are highly sought after by customers, given that the two are the largest companies in the world by revenue—customers are voting with their dollars. The loyalty rates for both these retailers are 90 per cent or greater, demonstrating high customer satisfaction and repeat purchase rates.

The value that these two formats offer to their shoppers can be organized under the four generic factors of time-saving, product assortment, price attractiveness and customer service (refer to Figure 4.1). In this discussion, we are ignoring the entertainment value or fun family outing benefits that physical stores provide, as we will explore this topic in Chapter 7. In addition, for the purposes of pictorial interpretation, we have made the differences between the retailers on the different value attributes in Figure 4.1 starker than they actually are.

The retailer's *time* value for a customer comprises waiting time (how long it takes to get the product), travel time and transaction time (the time taken to find the product, select/pick it up and checkout). At Walmart, the waiting time is determined by the closeness of a physical store to the customer. Given that 90 per cent of US shoppers now live within 10 miles

Figure 4.1. Amazon versus Walmart Value Proposition

	VALUE ATTRIBUTES	LOW VALUE	HIGH VALUE
TIME	Waiting time	A	W
	Travel time	W	A
	Transaction time	W	A
	Breadth	W	A
ASSORTMENT	Depth	W	A
	Brand choice	W	A
PRICE	Product price	A	W
	Delivery cost	A	W
	Travel cost	W	A
SERVICE	Assistance	A	W
	Ease of return	A	W
	Demonstration	A	W
	Recommendation	W	A
	Information	W	A

A: Amazon online; W: Walmart Supercenters

of a Walmart store, if the item is in stock, one can have the purchase in hand in half an hour. For Amazon, even with next-day delivery, there is a lag. One cannot rush out to get a carton of milk or an ingredient to complete a recipe in progress on Amazon and receive it right away.

However, we must distinguish physical products from digital ones, where the customer can download the product (e.g., e-books, music, hotel bookings, tickets for travel or entertainment, computer software). For digital products, Amazon online offers immediate consumption with no waiting time. Even with respect to physical products, Amazon is attempting, through local sub-depots, four-hour and same-day deliveries in densely populated areas for a small number of frequently ordered products, such as groceries.

On travel time (e.g., no need to leave home, dress up) and transaction time (especially after the one-click innovation),

Amazon is unbeatable. Walmart, with its large parking lots, huge stores and long lines at the cashier, cannot be competitive on these time attributes. Click and collect is Walmart's response to become more compelling on this front and lower its disadvantage vis-a-vis Amazon.

The *product assortment* offered by the retailer is measured by the breadth (number of product categories), brand choice (number of brands within a category) and depth (number of distinct SKUs within a brand in a category) available. While the largest Walmart Supercenters can be 2,60,000 square feet in the US—there is even a 1.2 million square foot Walmart in Zhuhai, China—they are still limited by physical space. Each store must make choices based on the neighbourhood it is located in, on what assortment to offer and which items not to stock.

One of Amazon's greatest advantages is the endless aisle, especially when offerings from the marketplace vendors are included. Without a physical space constraint, Amazon can easily include the long tail (those products that few customers desire, and therefore, take a long time to move from the 'shelf'), as it only needs to list the items from a third-party seller. A customer does not have to encounter futile drives to a store only to discover that either the retailer does not stock the item in question or has run out of it. Retailers, including Walmart, are trying to overcome these challenges to some extent by sharing real-time store inventory online. However, there will always be a lag, as an item may be in customers' shopping carts but not checked out yet. Only on checkout can the store inventory be updated. In any case, having real-time individual store inventory is still rare.

On *price attractiveness* or more comprehensive cost of product acquisition for the customer, one needs to consider product price, cost of delivery (the one which is charged to the shoppers) and the customer's cost of travel. Both retailers strive to offer the lowest product price. Many studies have examined which retailer is cheaper. While the answer depends on the product in question, in general, if only the product price is considered, Walmart usually wins if the customer is willing to go to the store and pick it up. In a comparison of prices of fifty identical items across a variety of categories such as home goods, technology and entertainment, and kitchen/appliance, one study found Amazon online to be 10.37 per cent more expensive than Walmart in-store.[6] Note, here we are comparing Amazon online with Walmart's physical store, not with the prices at Walmart's online store, where studies typically find Amazon online to be cheaper.[7]

Of course, Walmart's price guarantee ensures that the customer will pay the lowest price if this is brought to the attention of the retailer. Counter-intuitively, academic studies demonstrate that a price-match guarantee by a large retailer tends to result in higher prices for customers relative to the absence of such a price match. Why? In the face of a price-match guarantee, other retailers desist from price competition realizing the futility of this strategy since any reduction in prices will be immediately matched by the price guarantor. A price-match guarantee also effectively outsources to customers what is an impossible task for any brick-and-mortar retailer to achieve—checking prices at all competing stores for the thousands of SKUs it carries. While Amazon prices may be slightly higher (as Amazon must pick, assemble and deliver the order), there is no travel cost for customers involved with shopping at Amazon. However, customers do have to either pay for delivery or subscribe to Prime.

Related to the above is lot size; the principle at Walmart is that the higher the quantity, the greater the cost savings accrued. Unless it is a high-priced item, one will not drive to Walmart for a single item except when it is needed immediately. Convenience stores serve that need of immediate access to everyday necessities. Similarly, for a low-priced single item, Amazon delivery charges may be high. However, this is where Amazon Prime makes a big difference for the customer. Again, the buying situation (one item versus many, expensive basket versus cheap) and the location of the customer vis-a-vis Walmart have an impact on total customer acquisition cost. Regardless, both these retailers are highly competitive on price, with Walmart's physical store having an edge in sticker prices on physical products, especially when the shopper ignores travel costs.

Despite having the unique capability to do so, Amazon has not been able to practice differential pricing for different customers (price discrimination). Amazon has the data to determine the relative price sensitivity of individual customers based on past browsing and purchase history. Using this, their artificial intelligence engine could be programmed to offer different prices for the identical product simply based on who the customer is. However, attempts to do so in the past were found to be unacceptable to Amazon shoppers. This could be on account of the online medium being an open and transparent channel, accessible to all at any point in time. Yet, certain industries, like airlines, successfully offer different prices for the same seats depending upon the time they are being booked and the person's browser history.

The *customer service* aspect is a sum of many factors such as assistance by a salesperson, ease of return, demonstration capability (ability to touch, feel and try), personal recommendations and the extent of information available about the product. The brick-and-mortar model of Walmart enables it to provide personal assistance, an easier return process and a tangible product experience. Amazon tries to negate some of these disadvantages by offering a simple and free return process, but it is still a hassle for the customer.

In contrast, the online medium enables Amazon to provide not only detailed information about the product, personal recommendations and reviews from actual users but also a two-way platform to compare products and ask the seller specific questions. This Amazon advantage is now declining as consumers increasingly own a smartphone connected to the Internet via unlimited mobile data plans. If a shopper chooses to, as 70 per cent of US shoppers do, they can dig into their pockets and open any retail website, including Amazon, to access product information while shopping at a Walmart store.

Much of Amazon's advantage comes from the exhaustive data it has on customers. It can track shoppers from their social media streams, online search and past behaviour on its website. By collating and manipulating this data, Amazon obtains a comprehensive and rich picture of each of its customers. Equipped with this information, Amazon has the capability to achieve the ultimate level of micro-segmentation and customize its web page for every customer, recommending products most likely to be bought according to the individual's characteristics, needs and behaviour in the past.

Simply put, Amazon's big data analytics reveal the conditional probability of a shopper buying product B if they have bought product A. This process is known as collaborative filtering. When a shopper fires up the Amazon app or website, it presents the product(s) that have been bought by other shoppers with similar past purchase history, along with its reviews. Thus, while promotions at Walmart are driven by supplier push and broadcast to all shoppers entering the store at the same time, promotions at Amazon are driven by customer pull and customized for each individual shopper. Two customers logging in at the same time on Amazon will see entirely different landing pages or storefronts.

Walmart's access to customer data is limited to store-level analysis of the sales pattern through checkout receipts. The focus of Walmart is on identifying what products need to be stocked in a specific store based on the neighbourhood in which the store is located. Thus, a store in one neighbourhood (e.g., a high proportion of Hispanics) carries a product assortment that could be quite different from a store located in another neighbourhood (e.g., a campus town with a high proportion of university students).

The differential access to data ensures that while Walmart customizes its store based on the needs of the people who live in that locality, Amazon customizes its website page (Amazon store) based on the needs of an individual customer. The latter is obviously more powerful from a customer's perspective provided the customer is willing to ignore privacy concerns. Both companies have been and are pioneers in deploying information technology. They lead in the adoption of using data for managing their business but with rather different capabilities based on their distinctive mode of operation and business model.

From our discussion of Figure 4.1, one can conclude:

- The value proposition offered by the two retailers varies across different elements, with each offering higher value on certain elements and lower on others. It is important to note that on most factors, the two brands are at cross-purposes with each other, thus necessitating that customers make trade-offs when choosing one over the other. The two retailers aim to overcome the compromise shoppers have to make when they choose their channel versus the other. The important conclusion is that while the two retailers compete for customer dollars, the value curves demonstrate that customers see them as fulfilling complementary needs.
- The value curve can also be used to revisit the segmentation question. The difference between the two propositions is

not that they target different demographic segments (which will even be less so in future), but rather, different 'need' segments. When the consumer prefers the value curve of offline retail, then the default is Walmart, and when the consumer prefers the online proposition, Amazon has become the default. The unique selling proposition (USP) of the two retailers differ. Amazon is trying to improve its default status through Prime, as once the consumer pays the annual fee, there is no reason to look elsewhere on the web. Prime reduces the time of delivery as well so that unless there is an immediate need, it is good enough. This also explains the growing share of online relative to offline retail and the high market valuation of Amazon.

- Walmart's overall sales revenue is more than that of Amazon despite the former having a smaller global footprint, so it cannot be that a Walmart physical store is a less attractive proposition than Amazon online. More of the American population shops at Walmart than at Amazon. The typical shopper who is found at both retailers spends 13.5 per cent of their budget at Walmart and 11 per cent at Amazon. Furthermore, Walmart is rather profitable, while Amazon at best breaks even (even that is unlikely as we will see later in the book) on its retail sales (ignoring Amazon profits from AWS and advertising).

- Finally, different distribution channels offer different value propositions—to say one is better than the other is misguided (it is a situational preference, like a convenience store to a supermarket). Multichannel retailing has been the norm since the advent of modern retailing. For more than a century, the popularity of existing formats changed in the face of new retail formats. Think supermarkets taking over from mom-and-pop stores (currently reborn as convenience stores), discounters from supermarkets, malls from department stores and now online stores from brick-and-mortar stores. The older formats do not die, and may even grow in sales, but they become smaller in terms of their relative share of the total retail sales.

Role of Product Category in Driving Retail Preference

An important factor that drives customer adoption of online (Amazon) versus offline (Walmart) is the nature of the product category. In February 2021, music, videos, books and magazines commanded the highest online share at 69 per cent of the total category sales, followed by consumer electronics at 53 per cent, apparel at 38 per cent and food and beverage at only 4.8 per cent.[8, 9] As a result, we see a dramatic change in the composition of the main street (referred to as the high street in the UK) retail space over the past two decades. Many stores carrying books, videos and music have disappeared. Department stores that accounted for much of the apparel sales are fewer and smaller. Instead, coffee bars, beauty parlours and restaurants have become ubiquitous.

Despite their lower online penetration, apparel (total market estimated at $317 billion) and groceries (approximately $1.1 trillion) are two of the largest categories in the US.[10, 11] Observing this discrepancy, Jeff Bezos had remarked early in Amazon's history, 'In order to be a 200-billion-dollar company, we have got to learn how to sell clothes and food.'[12]

To explain differing penetration of online retail across books, apparel and groceries, we will examine the factors listed in Table 4.1. To reiterate, by doing so, we seek to reveal that customer behaviour and loyalty to brick-and-mortar stores versus online retail is not as clear-cut as saying 'physical stores are dead and the future is online'. Instead, in some categories (e.g., books), online is a more powerful proposition for

Table 4.1. Online versus Offline Fit with Product Categories

	Books	Clothing	Groceries
Assortment	Online long-tail availability adds value	Long tail adds some value, especially for more unique sizes	Long tail adds limited value as substitutable
Standardization	Yes, no differences in quality	Yes for staples, no for fashion items	No standardization as impossible for fresh items
Quality information	Superior online as reviews	Fit, fabric, colour superior offline	Superior offline as idiosyncratic
Returns	Not expected by customer	Many, need robust and easy return process	Difficult as perishable, so credit expected and dissatisfaction
Waiting time	Limited value of immediate delivery or digital delivery	Can wait, but excitement of buy now missing	List-driven but missing items problem
Unattended delivery	Possible, and low value	Possible, but valuable items	Impossible for frozen and fresh items
Prices	Lower online, delivery cost minimal	Delivery cost relatively small to order value but returns are costly	Delivery cost substantial as picking + poor value/volume ratio + complexity of fresh, frozen, ambient combinations

customers relative to physical stores, while in other product categories (e.g., groceries) offline offers a superior proposition.

Bezos started Amazon with books, and it was an inspired choice. When examining the power of selling books online versus going to a store to make the purchase, all the factors in Table 4.1—assortment, standardization, quality information, waiting time, unattended delivery, returns and prices—favour e-commerce. Not surprisingly, estimates suggest that Amazon accounts for 50 per cent of print book sales and 83 per cent of e-books sold in the US.

Assortment

The appropriate assortment for a retailer is a major decision. A long-tailed distribution of sales in retailing is one where many items that generate sales are far from the 'head' or the central part of the distribution. If the distribution of buying preferences of customers is long-tailed, it puts the online retailer at an advantage over the physical store. Digital retailers can afford to carry a larger assortment of items without facing the space constraints and inventory costs that a physical retail store does. Books are a classic long-tail category, where buyer preferences are diverse, with many niche titles and even out-of-print books desired by customers. Anyone wishing to become an author can self-publish, adding to the number of unique titles in the category.

A physical store like Walmart is forced to concentrate on the bestsellers so that they maintain adequate stock turns while optimizing their inventory and valuable retail space. If the product stays on the shelf for longer than optimal, it is hard to justify it occupying the shelf space. The primary point here is not that Amazon online can offer a larger assortment than Walmart's physical store, which is true regardless of category, but rather that a larger assortment in books is more attractive to consumers compared to other categories like apparel or groceries.

In contrast to books, apparel has a smaller long tail. While there are many manufacturers, most of the sales are in the popular sizes (S, M, L and XL). When it comes to groceries, the success of the hard discounters, like Aldi and Lidl, has demonstrated that 1000–1500 SKUs can complete the basket for many shoppers. In other words, stocking the long tail adds less value to groceries relative to books, with apparel falling somewhere in between.

Standardization

The standardization prevalent in the product category is an important driver of how comfortable consumers feel shopping online versus offline. For any particular book, there are generally a few options: hard cover, soft cover and e-book. The customer has a good idea of what they will receive, and all hardcovers of the same title are identical. In contrast, the perfect ripeness of an apple or a melon, according to one's preference, is difficult to ascertain online. There is no standard industry definition of 'ripe,' and in any case, what is considered ripe differs across customers and even for a customer, it depends on the intended end use (eat as a fruit or use to make jam). Consequently, for assessing the quality of fresh foods, the offline physical store is rated by customers to be far superior to the online experience.

With apparel, while there are standard industry sizes, not all designers and brands follow them precisely. A phenomenon called 'vanity sizing' is followed by some apparel brands, where they alter clothing sizes so that customers can vainly claim they are, for example, a size six when in reality, they are a size eight. It is supposed to make the shoppers feel better about themselves.

Reputedly, J.Crew, Gap and Banana Republic are brands where one must size down to get the correct size. While H&M and Levi's tend to offer average sizes, Zara and Abercrombie & Fitch run small or are more accurate relative to standard size charts.[13] Beyond these brand variances, in fashion merchandise, the cut of the design combined with the infinite variation in human bodies, especially for women, adds additional idiosyncrasies. Within the same designer's merchandise, a person may perfectly fit one size for a particular item but an adjacent size for a different item.

Quality Information

The extent of quality information available online of an item under purchase consideration differs by product category. A consumer shopping for books obtains superior information online. Beyond the reader reviews, the consumer can see similar, related books, sales rankings and detailed author pages, and the first chapter of the book may also be available to read for free—all this accessible from the comfort of their own home. In contrast, for apparel, quality information is superior in physical stores because of the tangible experience, whereby shoppers can see the colours, touch the fabric or try on the garment for fit and see how it will look when worn.

The prevalent standardization and a need for limited quality information for certain kinds of apparel predisposes them to be favoured by customers when buying online. Table 4.2 has the bestselling apparel items for men, women and children on Amazon.

It is apparent that customers are more willing to buy staples rather than fashion apparel online. In the industry, staple items are those that the customer buys regularly and which face a straight rebuy situation. Think of items such as innerwear, socks,

Table 4.2. Amazon US Top Selling Apparel Items

2021	Men's Apparel	Women's Apparel	Kid's Apparel
Top sub-category	Sleep & Loungewear	Sleep & Loungewear	Sleepwear
Top selling Item			
2017			
Top sub-category	Jeans	Innerwear	Girl's Basics
Top selling item			

Source: Amazon Website; and Lauren Thomas, 'Amazon and Target Are in a War over Apparel', CNBC, 15 February 2018, https://www.cnbc.com/2018/02/15/amazon-and-target-are-in-a-war-over-apparel.html, accessed June 2022.

dress shirts for men, sleepwear or basic jeans. Often, consumers have favourites for these items based on what they own. Being familiar with the brand they use and knowing the quality to expect, as well as confident of the size for that item, they find reordering it online easy. With T-shirts and sleepwear, especially for children, fit considerations are relatively unimportant—a bit larger is not a problem unlike for fashion items.

For fashion items that change every season with unique designs, the offline store is preferred. All the problems of assessing fit mentioned above come into play. As the items are new products, being offered for the first time, consumers need a lot more information to see if it is something they wish to buy. Physical stores offering tangible product experience with changing rooms to assess fit and quality are vastly superior from the shopper's perspective. This explains why one observes lines outside a changing room in Zara, with each person having four to six items of clothing in their hands. When they emerge from the changing room, they may purchase only a single item, with the rest discarded because they did not work for them.

The Problem of Returns

The standardization and quality information challenges as well as the lack of see, feel and touch, lead consumers to often perceive they have not received what they should have based on their onscreen experience. The average e-commerce return rate was between 20–30 per cent versus 8–10 per cent for brick-and-mortar stores. E-commerce returns in 2022 were estimated at $817 billion, and according to the National Retail Federation, the costs of these returns for the retailers amounted to $101 billion. Not only does the retailer bear the cost of delivery but it must also pay for the return logistics if the shopper decides not to keep the item.

The problem differs dramatically across categories. Returns are typically not a consideration for books, especially downloads. Even for physical books, consumers do not expect to return books unless the book is damaged in the shipping process. No one returns a book because they found the ending unsatisfactory or the book poorly written. Once bought, the consumer accepts it as a non-refundable purchase.

Groceries are more complicated, especially for perishable items. Dissatisfied customers expect a refund. Online retailers, considering the low value of individual items and the relatively substantial logistics cost of processing the physical return of the item, prefer to simply credit the customer and let them keep it. Data analytics can reveal the tiny percentage of shoppers who may abuse this system. The challenge for online retailers of groceries is that if, on an order of twenty grocery items, the online vendor fails to deliver a single item, customer dissatisfaction can run high as it may be an essential ingredient for the meal being prepared.

As expected, the percentage of online shoppers returning clothing is the highest at 26 per cent. Customers returning merchandise in categories closely associated with apparel, such as bags and shoes, are 19 and 18 per cent, respectively. In contrast, only 11 per cent of online shoppers return food and beverage items or books, movies and games (excluding downloads).[14] Understanding the challenge of selling fashion items online, e-commerce players like Amazon are increasingly allowing shoppers to order several items of clothing, try them on at home, retain what they wish and return the remaining items (no delivery charges either way).

If consumers are less than willing to pay the full cost of delivery, they are even more unwilling to pay for the returns. Recognizing the debilitating effects of returns on profitability, especially in the apparel category, some retailers are starting to adopt more restrictive policies. While only cult retailers can charge customers for returns, many retailers are attempting to limit returns in other ways. Amazon shortened the window during which holiday gifts and purchases could be returned. Some stores are now offering only store credit rather than cash to reduce returns.

Online retailers must be careful when setting return policies and drive a balance between profitability concerns and customer incentives. Retailers like Zara have begun charging for returns, but most retailers cannot as it reduces the incentive for customers to order online. The detrimental effects on sales volume force online apparel retailers to offer free and easy returns. Online shoppers often boast that they ordered six items of clothing when they only wished to buy one as the rest can be easily returned.

Stores offer cheaper and often preferred customer locations for returning an item. For a retailer, returns at its stores can generate substantial savings, depending on the return percentage of the product category (high in the case of clothes) and the percentage of shoppers opting for store returns. Also, returns to the store create opportunities for impulse or replacement sales. In contrast, warehouses cannot manage walk-in customer returns, given their relatively remote locations, and are set up to service delivery trucks via automated bays. Therefore, the warehouse pick model needs to develop a dedicated, efficient and customer-friendly returns process.

Positive approaches to reducing returns include ensuring that the size, fit and fabric information online is accurate, and the use of augmented reality tools to help the online shopper evaluate the items better. To reduce the cost of returns, Net-a-Porter is experimenting with waiting at the door while the customer tries on the apparel. By immediately returning unwanted merchandise to the delivery person, the return pickup trip is eliminated, although it results in a longer delivery time per order.

For small-value products, some retailers simply leave the merchandise with the shopper, preferring to give full credit rather than incur the additional cost of returns. The returns problem has attracted several players like Happy Returns, Ole and Returnly. A twist on Instacart, Ole allows shoppers to buy from stores via its app. Ole delivers the order, waits while the customer tries it on and takes back the returns, if any. No prizes for guessing the poor profitability of these business models.

Returns of online purchases often entail customers having to go through a tedious process of repackaging the unwanted item, printing out a label, waiting for the package to be collected and finally getting the refund. The time and the hassle involved in the process represent a paradox for e-retailing, which is centred on the promise of ease, convenience and flexibility. In a 2021 survey, 73 per cent of online shoppers indicated that the return experience affected their choice to purchase from a retailer again.[15] For retailers, not only do returns increase the logistical complexity of their online operations, but they also add considerably to the costs incurred. Since 62 per cent of the customers surveyed preferred in-store returns, physical store retailers (or online retailers with omnichannel presence) are at an advantage.[16]

Yet, Amazon is making inroads in apparel, especially in staples among those who prefer online shopping. A 2019 survey on online buying of apparel indicated that more than 50 per cent of respondents preferred Amazon, followed by nearly 34 per cent opting for Walmart online and about 25 per cent for brands' own websites.[17] When asked for reasons why they shopped for apparel on Amazon, 54 per cent of consumers mentioned free and fast shipping, 20 per cent lower prices and discounts, 16 per cent customer reviews and 13 per cent the ability to make easy returns.

Delivery and Waiting Time

When it comes to delivery, with digital books, it is immediate for the customer and costless for the online retailer. Even physical books are cheap to deliver because unattended delivery is possible, as they do not need to be refrigerated like groceries, are relatively low value compared to fashion items, and are rarely stolen from the lobby or the front door of an apartment. Unattended delivery combined with the lack of urgency to receive it allows for greater optimization of logistics (truck scheduling and routing) compared to delivering during a predetermined time slot when the shopper is present to take physical delivery.

Apparel merchandise tends to be of higher value, which requires that despite its ambient nature, online retailers must be careful to leave it in a secure location to avoid pilferage. Many new apartment complexes now have a secure locker system or space for leaving online deliveries. In general, the cost of delivering apparel is not large relative to the value of the merchandise. From the customer's perspective, e-commerce delivery systems can therefore satisfactorily deliver the merchandise and it is also cost-effective for the retailer. However, the excitement of 'getting it now' is missing, or if you have a party to go to that night and need to complete your outfit, then the physical store dominates the online proposition.

Delivering groceries against online orders is a complex as well as costly endeavour. It is in many ways the holy grail of e-commerce, no matter how much venture capital chases it. The problems are known. An average grocery order is of relatively low monetary value, high physical bulk and a mix of ambient, chilled and frozen products. There must be someone to receive the delivery so that the products can be immediately stored appropriately. Having to be present even for the pre-appointed time slot is inconvenient to the consumer and therefore Walmart online, with its click-and-collect option (something that Amazon, as an online retailer, cannot offer) in addition to delivery at home, is more competitive in this category. As a result, Walmart has a 32 per cent online grocery market share compared to Amazon's 29 per cent.[18] In contrast, for online apparel, Amazon's 38 per cent share dwarfs Walmart's 2 per cent.[19]

While we will explore retailer profitability of grocery delivery in the upcoming chapters, suffice it to say that from a customer perspective, shopping online for groceries is a much less compelling proposition relative to physical stores for all the reasons discussed above.

Our detailed deep dive into the valued customer and value proposition of Amazon online and Walmart physical stores reinforces the perspective of the previous chapters on the clash between these two retailers. Shopper needs demonstrate the reasons behind the existence of both formats. Depending on the mix of factors such as buying situation (e.g., need for immediate access to the product), product category (e.g., music versus groceries) and consumer preferences (e.g., price sensitivity), a shopper may patronize one format over the other. While Amazon and Walmart may seem to be racing towards an impending clash, and the press may play this facet up, the reality favours strategic complementarity between these two players based on their core competencies.

Chapter Takeaways

- Demographic differences between shoppers of Amazon and Walmart have collapsed as 95 per cent of Americans shopped at a Walmart last year and more than 70 per cent shopped at Amazon.
- Over time, almost all consumers will shop at both these retailers, seeking Walmart for the most competitive prices and Amazon for convenience. However, the preferences of shoppers between Amazon and Walmart depend on the need being fulfilled and the buying situation.
- For books, the online proposition, with its endless aisle, overwhelming product information, digital and unattended delivery possibilities, no need for returns and cheaper online

prices, leads Amazon to dominate Walmart. Physical book retail is a niche industry.

- For apparel, one must make the distinction between staples and fashion merchandise. Purchases of staples are increasingly moving online, especially for items (e.g., men's shirts, jeans and innerwear) that are a rebuy situation. For fashion items that change seasonally, physical stores are a more compelling proposition because of the ability to try on the merchandise before purchase. Attracted by the convenience, Amazon and other online fashion retailers are making headway, but at the cost of processing a lot of customer returns.

- For groceries, physical retailers like Walmart remain the preferred shopping destination for consumers. Online retailing in this category suffers from an inability to adequately communicate product characteristics, the inconvenience of having to be home to receive delivery and higher prices once delivery costs are included. The relatively greater attractiveness of click-and-collect for groceries also offers physical retailers like Walmart an advantage over pure e-commerce players, even when competing for online orders.

5

Is Online Retailing Profitable?

In the bustling village of Cybershore, a small online store named SparkNook thrived selling handmade crafts and unique artworks. The shop was run by a passionate young entrepreneur named Kadambari, who poured her heart and soul into curating a collection that celebrated creativity and individuality.

As orders poured in from across the digital landscape, Kadambari noticed a growing concern: the costs of delivering her products to customers were eating away at her profits. Each delicate art piece required special packaging, and the shipping fees added up quickly. Despite the increasing sales, SparkNook's profit margins remained slender.

One evening, as the sun set over the horizon, Kadambari sat down to contemplate the challenge. She realized that she was trapped in a delicate dance between making her customers happy with fast and reliable deliveries and ensuring her business remained financially sustainable. Something needed to change.

Kadambari realized the vast amounts of consumer data that was being collected could be analysed and used to create detailed profiles of individuals' preferences, behaviours and habits. She developed algorithms that predicted consumer desires and influenced purchasing decisions. The path to profitability lay in the monetization of this data. She discovered that other companies were willing to pay handsomely for insights into consumer behaviour. Advertisers, retailers and even governments sought to tap into this treasure trove of information to tailor their offerings and strategies.

The Wheel of Retailing

Retailing is an industry characterized by constant change. New retail formats and concepts emerge—of which online retailing is the latest one—while the existing formats fade away. In 1958, the wheel of retailing was proposed as an important hypothesis to explain retail evolution patterns.[1] The fundamental argument was that innovative new retail formats always start as low-margin, low-price, low-status operators, often with limited assortment—for example, the original Walmart discount store or Aldi. Over time, they gradually invest in more elaborate and expensive premises, furnishings and services, necessitating higher prices, which provides the opportunity for a new retail format to emerge that undercuts the original innovator's prices.

Traditionally, new retail formats have been delivering their price advantage through lower service levels. For example, Aldi provides a limited assortment, mostly their own private labels, in a bare shopping environment with no fixtures.[2] Usually, the supplier's outer case or carton in which products are delivered to the retailer is used for the merchandising display. The customer must bag their own groceries and pay a deposit to collect the shopping cart, ensuring that they return it to the appropriate place. This reduces the labour that Aldi needs, as shoppers do much of the work that is usually done by employees at supermarkets. Similarly, by leaving transportation and final assembly to the shopper, IKEA replaces employee costs with customer efforts.[3] Since IKEA originated in Sweden, a relatively high social cost country, the labour costs for a retailer were substantial. There was a strong incentive for shoppers to do it for themselves and in return, have IKEA pass on the cost savings through lower prices. The big takeaway here is that traditionally, retail innovation and low prices have been a result of customer labour replacing retailer labour.

At first glance, and the way it was sold to investors, Amazon and online retailing appear to fit the narrative of retail innovation at lower costs. In classroom discussions on Amazon, with executives or MBA students, the participants immediately note that relative to brick-and-mortar stores, Amazon benefits from no capital investment in physical stores and much lower inventory, given its ability to concentrate the stock in a few large warehouses versus hundreds, or even thousands, of stores that retail chains like Walmart need.[4] Furthermore, an online retailer has no merchandising or store operating costs. All the staff that are needed to provide service at traditional physical retailers are unnecessary, such as the 2 million-plus army of workers that service 10,000-plus Walmart stores worldwide. Given fewer assets (stores, inventory) and operating expenses (labour, merchandising), the reasonable expectation is that online retailing will be a financially lucrative business model with high margins and high return on assets. This, combined with the growth prospects, explains the trillion-dollar-plus market capitalization of Amazon.

Yet, a deeper exploration reveals that online retailing flies in the face of historical precedent and the 'wheel of retailing' hypothesis. Instead of offering lower prices by having shoppers participate more heavily in the marketing flows, e-tailers are offering greater service without a price penalty. The e-tailers pick the products from the shelves, pack them adequately for transport and then deliver them to the shopper's premises—all activities that shoppers previously did for themselves.

While some online retailers do charge something for delivery, customers in general seem resistant to paying the full costs of delivery. Why? First, shoppers are ignorant of the full costs of picking and delivery that a retailer pays. Second, customers perceive these logistical activities as being of low value because they do not place a large enough monetary value on their own labour and transportation costs. Third, competition between online retailers is often on how little shoppers will be charged for delivery and how fast they will receive their orders. This competitive dynamic has been enabled by lots of venture capital seeking to establish dominant positions, and thus, tolerating unprofitable last-mile delivery business models (e.g., DoorDash, Instacart, JustEat, Uber).

Overlooked in all this is that an online retailer like Amazon must invest large amounts of capital in building the last-mile delivery infrastructure to meet shoppers' expectations with respect to speed, certainty and accuracy of delivery as well as manage a convenient process for returns. Furthermore, these delivery costs must be recouped from relatively small orders in terms of dollar value and in categories that typically yield small dollar margins for the retailer. We will see that while Amazon's online retail is perceived as a high-tech business, it may simply be a capital-intensive, low-margin, physical logistics business!

A Deep Dive into Amazon Profitability

The original Amazon idea, before AWS (their cloud computing business), advertising (charging vendors to plug their products on Amazon website), or Marketplace (third-party sellers using the Amazon website for sales in return for a commission paid to Amazon), was to be a pure online retailer. Online retailing meant Amazon would buy products from suppliers, keep inventory, sell to customers via its website and then deliver. This e-tail concept was what initially excited investors and resulted in Amazon's worldwide iconic brand status. However, now, pure online retail revenues are less than half of Amazon's total revenues (see Table 5.1).

Table 5.1. Breakdown of Amazon Revenues

Revenues in USD million	2016	2021	2022
AWS (cloud computing services)	12,219	62,202	80,096
Other (mostly advertising)*	2,950	33,336	41,986
Marketplace (commissions from third party vendors plus service fees)	22,993	1,03,366	1,17,716
Physical stores**		17,075	18,963
Subscriptions (Amazon Prime)	6,394	31,768	35,218
Online Retail	91,431	2,22,075	2,20,004
Total Amazon Revenues	1,35,987	4,69,822	5,13,983

*Amazon only reported advertising separately since 2021
** Physical stores revenues not meaningful prior to Whole Foods acquisition
Source: Annual reports

When Amazon ventured into cloud computing (AWS) in 2006, as previously noted in Chapter 3, observers saw it as a distraction. Markets were less than enamoured, as exemplified by the headline in Businessweek, 'Amazon's Risky Bet'. The magazine cover screamed, 'CEO Jeff Bezos wants to run your business with his Web technology. Wall Street wishes he would just mind the store'.[5] Yet, since 2014 (until and including 2022), when Amazon started reporting AWS results separately, the operating income from AWS accounted for 83 per cent ($81 billion out of $98 billion) of Amazon's total operating income. For three financial years (2014, 2017, 2022), the operating income of AWS exceeded Amazon's total operating income. Consider that for the most recent year, 2022, operating income from AWS operations was $22.8 billion, while the total operating income for Amazon was only $12.2 billion. This implies a loss of over $10 billion from the non-AWS operations of Amazon. Clearly, AWS is a big part of how they have financially survived and scaled up.

In contrast, when Amazon opened its website to third-party vendors (Marketplace) in 2000, it was well-received. Marketplace is now a large and lucrative operation, with revenues from commissions and services from third-party vendors exceeding $117 billion in 2022. Advertising was something that never excited Jeff Bezos. It was as recently as 2021 that Amazon reported its advertising revenues separately for the first time. The point is that much of the enthusiasm for Amazon has been founded on the potential of its online retail operations, and since that is also the focus of this book, let us examine Amazon's profitability from its online sales in depth. And, for the purposes of this exercise, we will focus on the North American operations.

Investigating the profitability of online retailing in North America will help discern whether Amazon (the largest, best, most experienced online retailer in the world) can generate profits from online retail sales in the largest and arguably the most advanced e-commerce market in the world. Furthermore, as per Table 5.2, since Amazon was unprofitable in the most recent financial year of 2022 (if one ignores AWS), we will work off the profitable 2021 performance. We are biasing our selection to obtain the rosiest picture of Amazon's online retail profitability. If Amazon, after almost thirty years of operations, is unable to break even on its online retail business in its best market, then it is unlikely that others can do better.

Table 5.2. Amazon 2022 and 2021 Results

In USD million	2021 Revenues	2022 Revenues	2021 Operating Income	2022 Operating Income
North America/USA	2,79, 833	3,15,880	7,271	-2,487
International	1,27,787	1,18,007	-924	-7,746
Amazon Web Services	62,202	80,096	18,532	22,841
TOTAL	4,69,822	5,13,983	24,879	12,248

Source: Amazon Annual Reports

Annual reports of companies are interesting documents. Purportedly, they are supposed to reveal to investors how the company is performing. In reality, annual reports attempt to obfuscate where and how the firm is making money to give managers greater flexibility to fudge numbers and avoid revealing vital information to competitors. Amazon is no exception. A simple query—what are the online retail sales of Amazon in North America?—is not available from the financial disclosures and therefore must be estimated. Only then can one proceed to answer the question: Does Amazon break even in its North American online retail business, ignoring AWS, advertising and Marketplace operations?

Table 5.3 presents the analysis to derive estimates of revenues and operating income for different parts of Amazon's North American operations in 2021. We know from the annual report that ignoring AWS (Table 5.2), Amazon's revenues and operating income worldwide were approximately $407 (469–62) billion and $6.3 (24.8–18.5) billion, respectively. The worldwide revenues from physical stores ($17 billion), Marketplace ($103 billion), Prime subscriptions ($32 billion), other (mostly advertising, $33 billion) and online retail ($222 billion) are also directly from the reported 2021 financials

Table 5.3. Estimate of Amazon's US Online Sales and Profits 2021

In USD billion	Worldwide Revenues*	NA/USA Revenues	Estimated Operating Income NA/USA	Comparable Business Model (margin***)
Physical Stores (Whole Foods)	17*	17 Primarily NA	0.8	Walmart Business Model (5%)
Third Party (commissions and services charged by Amazon to Marketplace vendors)	103*	70**	20.0	Alibaba Business Model (29%)
Subscriptions (Prime memberships)	32*	21**	Exclude as it supports e-tail	Netflix Business Model (21%)
Other	33 (of which 31 billion is advertising)*	22**	7.0 (more likely14)	Google Business Model (31%)
Online Retail (non-third-party online sales of Amazon)	222*	150**	-20.5 (more likely -27.5)	Pure e-tail Business Model
Total Amazon less AWS	407*	280*	7.3*	

* From annual report 2021

** We have assigned 67 per cent of the overall sales for each line of business to North America. This proportion was derived by taking the overall North America sales not including AWS of $280 billion from Table 1, deducting $17 billion for physical stores sales, which are assumed to be all North America. The remaining $263 billion for North America is 67 per cent and the $128 billion for international sales not including AWS is 33 per cent.

***Estimate based on comparable business model

Source: Amazon Annual Report 2021 and author estimates

(Table 5.1). What is not revealed is the breakdown of revenues between North America and the rest of the world for each of the different parts (e.g., Marketplace, online retail and advertising) of Amazon. Nor do we have the operating income, worldwide or North America, for the different Amazon businesses.

The physical stores business of $17 billion revenues is mostly from Whole Foods in North America. If we remove that from the revenues in Table 5.3, it indicates that North America accounts for about 67 per cent ($263 billion divided by $390 billion) of Amazon's non-AWS and non-physical stores revenues. In the absence of more accurate information, we can allocate two-thirds of the total revenues from the different business lines to North America. As a result, the North American revenues from physical stores, third parties, Prime subscriptions, other and online retailing are estimated at approximately $17, $70, $21, $22 and $150 billion, respectively (Table 5.3). Of course, these are not the actual numbers, but good enough for a judgement-based exercise to understand the profitability of the different businesses for Amazon. Whether the online retail sales of Amazon in North America are $135 billion or $165 billion will not matter to our conclusions. The point is that about a third of the revenues of the company come from online retailing in North America.

While we have estimates of revenues, we do not have any information about the profitability of these different businesses. As per Table 5.2 and Amazon's financial disclosures, the total operating income of Amazon in North America, excluding AWS, was $7.3 billion for 2021. This is the sum of the profits generated by the different lines of business. To make informed estimates, let us take a company whose business model (as shown in the last column of Table 5.3) best represents the line of business. For example, the physical store follows a 'Walmart type' business model and probably has an operating margin of

5 per cent. Thus, one can assume it accounts for $0.8 billion (5 per cent of $17 billion sales) of North American Amazon income. That leaves $6.6 billion (7.3–0.8) of 2021 operating income to explain from the rest of the North American businesses.

Third-party commissions and services from Marketplace are an 'Alibaba type' business model. Presumably, this must be a profitable business as Amazon is simply skimming the commissions of third-party GMV and booking them as Marketplace revenues. When Amazon does provide these Marketplace vendors with any logistical support, they probably charge the full cost as services. Not surprisingly, Alibaba, which follows this business model, makes a healthy 29 per cent of revenues as operating income from its China e-commerce business. Extrapolating that, Amazon North America probably generated $20 billion in income (29 per cent of $70 billion) from its Marketplace operations for the financial year 2021.

'Other' is primarily advertising and a 'Google-type' business model. In 2022, for the first time, Amazon revealed that its revenues from advertising for the financial year 2021 were over $31 billion, up 32 per cent from the previous year. While Google's operating margins are 31 per cent, Amazon should be even more profitable than Google as it does not need to invest in search. As mentioned previously, it is simply selling existing customers' past purchases and browsing data to advertisers. Past purchase data is also more likely to lead to conversion than demographic data at Meta or the contextual information of Google, and conversion is what drives advertising revenues. As a result, taking Google as the profitability benchmark, Amazon should have generated at least $7 billion (31 per cent of $22 billion) in operating income from the 'other business' in North America. If we consider the greater effectiveness and lower costs at Amazon of advertising, my own estimate would be more like $14 billion (62 per cent of $22 billion) of operating income in 2021.

Prime subscription is a 'Netflix-type' business model. However, one could argue that Amazon Prime is in support of the online retail business, so let us club subscription revenues and online retail sales to understand the profitability of this segment. As computed here, the physical stores ($0.8), third-party transactions ($20) and other ($7 or $14) businesses in North America together generate $27.8 billion, perhaps as high as $34.8 billion, in operating income versus the $7.3 billion overall for North America reported in Tables 5.2 and 5.3. This implies that the online business is losing at least $20.5 billion (7.3–27.8), more likely as high as $27.5 billion (7.3–34.8), on revenues of $171 billion ($150 billion online retailing plus $21 billion Prime), or a negative margin of approximately 12–16 per cent.

Some readers will find this profitability analysis astonishing, and those who consider Jeff Bezos to be god may even disagree with the numbers. Others, as participants in seminars often do, may argue that once the business scales up, profits will appear for Amazon. However, the data is not so supportive. First, Amazon has been in business for almost thirty years. Second, it is already by far the largest online retailer in the US and the economies of scale are yet to kick in. Third, and perhaps most damning, the fulfilment (picking, packing and shipping online orders) cost as a percentage of sales over the past fifteen years has gone in the wrong direction. In other words, in contrast to the top-down analysis above, a bottom-up profitability analysis based on delivery costs reinforces the financially losing proposition that online retailing is for Amazon. This bottom-up analysis of fulfilment costs is where we focus next.

Amazon Delivery Cost Analysis

For an online retailer like Amazon, fulfilling the shoppers' orders in a timely, accurate and cost-efficient manner is crucial.

Not only is delivery the essence of their value proposition to customers, their raison d'être, but also a fundamental driver of operating costs, profitability and the viability of the business model. Realizing the importance of the last-mile challenge, Amazon, more than any other online company, has invested enormous efforts and resources into building the fulfilment infrastructure of warehouses, picking systems, packaging solutions and transportation options. In pursuit of efficiency and customer satisfaction, as detailed in the next chapter, Amazon has led innovations and experiments in last-mile delivery for online shoppers. Despite this, as the analysis that follows will demonstrate, the financials for delivery are daunting.

Amazon reports the costs of delivery under the two buckets of fulfilment and shipping costs. Fulfilment costs for Amazon comprise primarily the operating and staffing costs of fulfilment centres, customer service centres and physical stores. On the other hand, shipping costs include both inbound and outbound shipping. As Table 5.4 indicates, Amazon's total delivery cost (fulfilment + shipping) as a percentage of sales declined from 24 per cent in 2001 to 17 per cent in 2006. One could attribute this to classic economies of scale, with Amazon getting greater efficiency and better rates (shipping was outsourced by Amazon during this period) as the volume of deliveries increased. Sales over the same period had grown threefold. However, from 2006 to date, total delivery costs as a percentage of sales have deteriorated, consistently and rather dramatically.

Between 2006 and 2022, as Table 5.4 shows, Amazon's delivery costs as a percentage of its overall revenues have almost doubled from 17 per cent to 32.65 per cent, despite annual sales revenues increasing about fifty times. On reflection, AWS and advertising ('other') being digital businesses do not contribute significantly, or anything, to the logistics costs incurred by Amazon. Thus, for a true picture of delivery costs as a percentage

Table 5.4. Amazon Delivery Cost Evolution

In USD million	2001	2006	2011	2016	2021	2022
Sales	3,122	10,711	48,077	1,35,987	4,69,822	5,13,983
Fulfilment costs	374	937	4,576	17,619	75,111	84,299
Shipping costs	376	884	3,989	16,200	76,700	83,500
Total delivery costs	750	1,821	8,565	33,819	1,51,811	1,67,799
Fulfilment costs as % of sales	11.98%	8.75%	9.52%	12.96%	15.99%	16.40%
Shipping costs as % of sales	12.04%	8.25%	8.30%	11.91%	16.33%	16.25%
Total delivery costs as % of sales	24.02%	17.00%	17.82%	24.87%	32.31%	32.65%
Amazon Prime subscribers	Millions	NA	4	65	200	200
Sales of AWS + Other				15,169	95,538	122,082
Amazon sales less AWS and Other				1,20,818	3,74,284	3,91,901
Delivery costs as a % of Amazon sales less AWS and Other				27.99%	40.56%	42.82%

Fulfilment costs are operating costs of running fulfilment centres, customer service centres and physical stores. Shipping costs include inbound and outbound shipping. One may argue that a more accurate computation of delivery costs as a percentage of sales would remove the operating costs of physical stores (around $16 billion) from the delivery costs and remove the $17 billion revenues of physical stores from the sales of Amazon. However, this would not change our conclusions as 32.31 per cent delivery costs as a percentage of sales would drop to only 30 per cent for 2021.

of sales, one should strip out the revenues of AWS and 'other' businesses. As the last row of Table 5.4 reveals, doing this results in delivery costs exceeding 40 per cent of online retail (Marketplace + online retail + Prime sales) revenues! For the purposes of this calculation, we have left Marketplace revenues (third-party commissions and services) untouched as Amazon does provide delivery support to its Marketplace vendors for a charge. However, this analysis can only be done for the most recent years, since Amazon has started reporting AWS and 'other' business revenues separately.

What explains the dramatic change in Amazon's delivery costs, from declining as a percentage of revenues until 2006 to increasing as a percentage of revenues since 2006? In a word: Prime. Before the introduction of Amazon Prime, which provides free unlimited deliveries for an annual subscription fee, shoppers had to pay a delivery fee with each order. As a result, consumers bundled their needs and ordered only when there were enough items in the basket to justify the fixed delivery charge per order. For Amazon, this meant greater efficiency— fewer delivery trips and larger individual orders.

With Amazon Prime, subscriber behaviour changed. Now, a shopper simply orders as the need arises, with no incentive to bundle the items. When your child requires a pen or you need dental floss, you simply order it on Amazon, and the next day, as few as three pens or six packs of dental floss show up. There is no incentive for a customer to bundle small orders or go to the store if one can wait for a day. These orders, with a value of less than $10, are delivered to the customer's home. Such small orders kill picking, and especially delivery, economics. Delivering a $10 pack of pens or a $1000 iPhone, from an absolute dollar picking, packing and shipping costs perspective, is not that different. Yet, the revenue and operating margin in dollars for the online retailer are dramatically so.

Moreover, it is from this absolute dollar margin per order that the online retailer must bear the dollar delivery cost per order. As the number of Prime subscribers between 2011 and 2021 increased from 4 million to 200 million, the economics of delivery deteriorated. Consistent with our conclusions, or perhaps even worse, a study by Morgan Stanley estimated that for one-day shipping, the typical Amazon order is $8.32, while Amazon spends $10.59 to fulfil and ship it![6]

Given the worsening delivery economics, one may wonder about the logic of introducing Amazon Prime. However, consumer research indicated that the biggest reason that people hesitated to order from Amazon was the delivery charge. A subscription removes this from consideration, and as a result, makes Amazon the default online retailer for the subscriber. Having paid for the annual subscription, the consumer, when in need of a specific product, does not search for another online retailer. Prime is Amazon's competitive advantage and gives its online retail business incredible 'stickiness'. Amazon has become the Google of shopping.

On the other hand, from a financial perspective, gross margins (the price shoppers pay for a product minus what Amazon pays its suppliers), as we saw from the Walmart analysis in Chapter 2, are around 25 per cent in this business. Simply considering the delivery costs of 40+ per cent, this means a negative margin of 15 per cent for the online retailing business. However, Amazon does have other costs of running its online operations apart from logistics costs. Assuming even a small 10 per cent of sales for other operating costs makes for a 25 per cent negative margin (40 per cent fulfilment + 10 per cent other operating costs—25 per cent gross margin) on online retail for Amazon. This is higher than the 12–16 per cent negative margin we computed using our top-down approach for 2021. Regardless, online retailing is a significant loss leader for Amazon. And this is for the North American operations; the rest of the world's economics will look much worse given the overall losses of overseas operations at Amazon.

The numbers for the most recent financial year, 2022, do not look any better and demonstrate a continuation of the trend. Amazon spent an eye-popping $167.8 billion on delivery, more than the GDP of 150 countries in the world (Kuwait, ranked fifty-nine, had a GDP of $164 billion),[7] 32.65 per cent of its $514 billion sales that year. Stripping away the AWS and 'other' revenues led to 42.82 per cent being expended to run delivery operations in support of the online retail and Marketplace sales. Since Amazon is the second largest company in the world based on revenues after Walmart, one must be sceptical of any scale-based arguments as the path to profitability for online retail, especially when the percentage of revenues spent on delivery is increasing rather than decreasing over the years. Removing the physical stores' revenues and operating costs from this analysis of delivery costs as a percentage of sales, while more accurate, strictly speaking, would not change any of our conclusions as physical stores are insignificant at less than 4 per cent of Amazon revenues (see footnote to Table 5.4).

Amazon versus Walmart Productivity Analysis

The operating costs of delivery are one aspect of the financials for Amazon. One must also consider the capital investment needed to build the delivery infrastructure. As noted earlier, it is presumed that Amazon will have much better ratios than a physical store chain such as Walmart with respect to employee productivity (sales per employee), inventory turns (sales to inventory) and asset turnover (sales to total assets).

Table 5.5 presents the data comparing Amazon to Walmart from 2001 to 2022. We can draw several conclusions from this

Table 5.5. Amazon and Walmart Productivity

	2001		2006		2011		2016		2021		2022	
	Amazon	Walmart	Amazon	Walmart	Amazon	Walmart	Amazon	Walmart	Amazon	Walmart	Amazon	Walmart
Sales (million USD)	3,122	217,799	10,711	344,992	48,077	443,854	135,987	481,317	469,822	567,762	513,983	611,289
Employees (000)	7.8	1,383	13.9	1,900	56.2	2,000	341.4	2,300	1,600	2,300	1,541	2,100
Inventory (million USD)	144	22,749	877	33,685	4,992	40,714	11,461	43,046	32,640	56,511	34,405	56,576
Total assets (million USD)	1,637	83,451	4,363	151,193	25,278	193,406	83,402	198,825	420,459	244,860	462,675	243,457
Sales/Employee (USD)	400,256	157,483	770,576	181,575	855,463	221,927	398,322	209,268	293,639	246,853	333,539	291,090
Sales/Inventory ratio	21.68	9.57	12.21	10.24	9.63	10.90	11.87	11.18	14.39	10.05	14.94	10.80
Sales/Inv. adjusted ratio*							8.54		8.35		7.97	
Sales/Assets ratio	1.91	2.61	2.45	2.28	1.90	2.29	1.63	2.42	1.12	2.32	1.11	2.51

Adjusted strips AWS, Other and Marketplace revenues out of Amazon's sales to compute the sales to inventory ratio. It can only be computed since 2016 as Amazon did not report the breakout numbers before then.

Source: Annual Reports and author estimates

analysis. Amazon's sales-to-employee ratio improved between 2001 and 2011 but started deteriorating after that. This was due to a massive increase in the logistics workforce. Similarly, Amazon's sales-to-total assets improved from 2001 to 2006 but started deteriorating after that rather dramatically. This was the effect of increased logistics investments such as warehouses and trucks, as the number of Prime subscribers climbed to over 200 million. Amazon was now a delivery business.

In contrast, Amazon's sales-to-inventory ratio deteriorated from 2001 to 2011 but started improving steadily after that. A closer examination reveals that this was primarily a function of the changing business composition of Amazon's overall revenues. AWS, Marketplace and advertising revenues have become a larger proportion of Amazon revenues compared to online retail. To make an accurate assessment of Amazon inventory turns, one should exclude revenues from AWS, advertising and Marketplace as Amazon does not carry any physical inventory on their books to support these businesses. Doing so drops Amazon's sales to inventory ratio from 14.39 to 8.35 for 2021, and further to 7.97 for 2022. When compared to Walmart's inventory turn ratio of 10.8, it is truly remarkable that a physical store chain with 10,000-plus stores can beat an online retailer on this metric.

At the outset, Amazon's advantages are touted as not requiring the same intensity of assets, inventory or employees relative to a physical store chain. This is supposedly what makes online retailing such an attractive business model. That is why it is amazing that Amazon is now close to Walmart on sales per employee ($3,37,432 vs $2,91,090) and as a pure retailing operation (ignoring AWS, advertising and Marketplace), worse on inventory turns (7.97 vs 10.8) and most surprisingly, much worse on asset turnover (1.11 vs 2.51). Moreover, if you look at the trend over the past ten years, Amazon's ratios are getting worse on all three of these metrics. Amazon, no matter its fame for exceptional execution, is a terribly run business when it comes to capital efficiency by traditional standards. Admittedly, this profitability and productivity analysis has been a judgement exercise. However, the perceptive reader will understand why Amazon makes it so hard to find these numbers. In the next chapter, we will examine how the logistics infrastructure is driving large capital investments.

Understanding Online Delivery Economics

Nothing above should lead us to conclude that online retail cannot be profitable. One needs to be nuanced in assessing the profitability of e-commerce. In general, there are four types of product categories marketed online, and each has different delivery economics driving it. Only an in-depth understanding of these economics will lead to the right conclusions on the viability of a particular online retail business model.

The first category is digital products such as music, e-books, movies, airline tickets and most banking transactions. These products can be delivered online to the consumer and there are no delivery costs to be considered. It is a fixed-cost business with essentially zero marginal costs for both the manufacturer (except for the royalty to the creator) and the retailer. Whether one sells one copy or a million copies of an album, it only has to be loaded on to the server once, from where the shoppers download it. Consequently, travel agents, music stores, book retailers and bank branches that used to be ubiquitous on the high street are fast disappearing. It is natural for consumers to migrate online for these digital product categories, as the channel proposition is so much more powerful than that of the retail stores. For online retailers, these digital products are a natural fit for their business and highly profitable.

The second category includes products that are large in terms of physical volume and where the shopper is used to paying for delivery in the offline retail context. Most white goods (e.g., refrigerators, stoves, washers and dryers), large brown goods (e.g., big screen televisions, home entertainment systems) and large furniture items (e.g., beds, mattresses, dining tables) fall in this category. Since these products do not fit in the vehicles of most shoppers and may require assembly on delivery as well as removing the packaging materials and old items, shoppers have always paid an additional charge that compensated the retailer for this delivery service. As a result, customers are psychologically prepared to pay almost the full cost of delivery. Of course, as in the offline world, online retailers may also subsidize delivery to some extent, but then this subsidy is built into their product margins.

The online channel proposition is less powerful for these bulky items as many shoppers prefer to touch, feel and see these products before purchase. Yet, because of showrooming, sales are increasingly moving online. Showrooming is the phenomenon of shoppers examining the merchandise in a traditional brick-and-mortar store and subsequently purchasing it online. Consequently, brick-and-mortar retailers are forced to match online prices for such products. While these products are expensive to deliver because of volume, weight and the need for careful handling, online sales are still profitable. As the dollar order size is relatively large, the dollar margin generated is adequate relative to any additional delivery costs beyond what the shopper is required to pay as delivery fees.

The third category of products are those where the absolute dollar margin generated per order is more than adequate to compensate the retailer for 'free' delivery, especially if the products are ambient and do not require special logistics. For example, apparel, luxury products or expensive wines and spirits. A luxury brand bag may be priced at $2000 with a retail margin of 30 per cent, generating a $600 gross margin on the sale. Even if the product is delivered by the retailer in a limousine by a white-gloved chauffeur, it would still be a profitable order. From the customers' perspective, while they enjoy shopping for such products as well as prefer the opportunity to touch, feel and see, there are situations where online shopping is favoured, like when gifting or buying a product that is familiar to the consumer.

The last category consists of products that have a combination of the following characteristics: low dollar order value, small gross margins, bulky items in terms of volume and/or weight, complicated delivery logistics and requiring the presence of the customer to receive delivery. Supermarkets and much of Amazon's sales, especially from its Prime subscribers, fall into this category, which explains the high delivery costs the retailer incurs. While loved by shoppers for the convenience offered without an adequate price penalty, online retailers are challenged to make money on such sales.

Grocery is the quintessential example of this category, and as such, one may declare that online grocery retailers will not be profitable in the foreseeable future. Why? The low margins, small average order size of the industry and the nature of grocery products, in addition to consumers' price sensitivity and delivery preferences, lead to significant economic and logistical challenges for retailers in offering an attractive but profitable online proposition. Yet, given the size of the opportunity, retailers continue to experiment with alternative delivery models in their search for a sustainable model for online grocery retail.

Amazon recognized that the focus of its growth strategy should be to more deeply penetrate the grocery and apparel categories, which boasted retail sales of $1.1 trillion and $317 billion, respectively, in 2021. The complexity involved in delivering groceries, and in handling the high percentage of returns in the case of apparel, has resulted in the two categories still skewed heavily towards offline retail, with groceries being especially problematic.

How Do You Solve a Problem Like Groceries?

Consumers are relatively price-sensitive with respect to online grocery prices as well as the delivery fee. Only 1 per cent of online grocery shoppers are willing to cover the full cost of delivery.[8] Any increase in delivery fee per order results in consumers placing less frequent large orders. While this does help retailer economics by generating more gross margin dollars per order, it reduces the overall volume since one obtains a lower share of the consumer wallet. Shoppers tend to do top-up shopping at offline stores between their infrequent large orders. Regardless, the delivery fee charged per order must still be a relatively small amount as there are always competitors willing to undercut this. Subscription models, as we observed with Amazon Prime, are not a solution. They simply incentivize shoppers to place many small orders, with severely detrimental effects on order economics for the retailer.

The grocery basket, while large in terms of volume and weight, has a relatively low dollar value. The average order size for someone purchasing online groceries was $85 in 2021.[9] This is for the US; in other countries, except perhaps for a few Western European nations, this number would be lower. Still, assuming an average order of $85, the gross margin dollars generated per order for the retailer will be around $21 (at 25 per cent gross margin for retailers). In general, the net margin for most supermarkets, after deducting the retailer's operating costs from the gross margin, ranges between 3 and 5 per cent, or $4 on an order of $85.

Traditionally, the major operating costs for offline retailers have been staff, rental, utilities and advertising. These costs are relatively fixed in the near term. Shoppers who come to the store bear the costs of assembling their basket from the shelves and transporting it home. In contrast, for online orders with home delivery, the retailer needs to pick, pack, assemble and deliver the order. Estimates vary, but fulfilling online orders costs the retailer, on average, $12–20 per order.[10] With $21 as the gross margin being generated per order and $4 as the net margin per order, the cost of delivery, even net of any delivery charges paid by online shoppers, kills the offline retailer's ability to make money on online orders.

It is important to remember that the above numbers are on average. The gross margin dollars generated per order as well as the fulfilment costs vary with the mix of brands and products comprising the order. For example, large bulky items or frozen items are more expensive to deliver for the retailer. Therefore, while both multipack carbonated drinks and fresh fish yield similar high gross margins for the retailer, the fulfilment costs for the bulky carbonated drinks multipack are considerably higher. Similarly, while both yoghurt and frozen vegetables generate relatively smaller gross margins for the retailer, the cost of handling and shipping the latter is higher.

Beyond the above, there is also the adverse selection problem. Some shoppers are prone to ordering bulky items online from strong brands, like cases of Coca-Cola, Evian bottled water, Scott's paper towels, P&G diapers and so on. In such cases, the retail gross margin dollar shrinks considerably, to perhaps as low as 12 per cent or $10 on an average order, while the delivery (picking plus transportation) costs of such bulky items are high. There is no path to profitability on home delivery of such products, and increasingly, online retailers (e.g., Amazon and Ocado in the UK) are limiting the number of such items allowed within a single order.

The other problem with grocery delivery is that a typical order has three types of items that warrant three different distribution chains: ambient (e.g., soaps, shampoos and toilet paper); chilled (e.g., milk, fruits and vegetables); and frozen (e.g., meats and ice cream). An average grocery order will have items from all three types, and hence, unlike a durable product such as a book, these groceries cannot be left outside if no one is at home at the time of delivery. While the ambient items are durable, the chilled and frozen items are perishable and are easily spoilt if not kept in the right conditions. In addition, the delivery process would entail higher costs as the truck that carries groceries would need to have suitable compartments for each type. It would also need more time, as the delivery person would have to take a bag out of each of the compartments—bag A, bag B and bag C—and ensure that all three belong to the same order before delivery.

Furthermore, in contrast to a book that can be left unattended in the apartment lobby or mailbox, someone must be home to receive the groceries. Therefore, customers prefer either faster delivery (e.g., within four hours) or certainty of delivery (e.g., a predefined one-hour slot within a few days). The more retailers accommodate customer delivery preferences, the higher the order fulfilment costs are. Faster delivery and promised delivery slots make route planning less efficient for delivery trucks and have a detrimental impact on the utilization of picking staff. Attended delivery also increases the contact time (e.g., wait for the customer to answer the door, take the elevator up to the apartment, place the groceries in the customer's preferred spot at home, some minimal chit-chat and return of plastic bags from previous orders).

All these factors make grocery deliveries a logistical nightmare for retailers. This is well-known among experts—

97 per cent of 500 supply chain executives surveyed declared current grocery delivery models 'unsustainable'.[11] Traditional brick-and-mortar retailers, familiar with the relative economics of delivering online orders versus having customers shop at the store, find it hard to get excited about the e-commerce business or even about click and collect. They are being forced into it because of customer demand but retailers know it is earnings-dilutive. Simon Roberts, Sainsbury's CEO, observed that with online orders, they were 'moving sales out of our most profitable convenience channel and driving a huge step-up in online grocery participation, our least profitable channel'.[12]

Since fulfilling such orders is a losing proposition on a variable cost basis (gross margin dollars generated per order minus delivery cost dollars per order), the more such online orders they fulfil, the more money online retailers lose! If a supermarket was previously doing 2 per cent of its business online and now starts doing 15 per cent, that helps it keep revenues from declining, but it will be at the expense of profitability. We reiterate what we said at the beginning of this chapter: online retailing is replacing what used to be customer labour with retailer labour, but the additional retailer costs are not being compensated through adequate delivery charges to customers.

Despite the poor economics of online orders, customer and investor demands have led leading online retailers worldwide to significantly ramp up their investments to provide customers with two key fulfilment models: the click-and-collect model, whereby online shoppers pick up groceries from a neighbourhood store, and the home delivery model, which provides the last-mile connectivity.

It is not surprising that retailers with a large physical network prefer their online shoppers to click and collect from the store. This restricts the retailer's fulfilment costs to picking and packing the order as the consumer transports the order home. It also creates in-store opportunities for cross-selling. Accurate public data on the profitability of online grocery orders is challenging to find. The estimates presented on online grocery profit margins worldwide by different fulfilment strategies that seemed most reasonable to me were by Statista.[13] They computed that if the grocer picks from the store, the profit margin is -15 per cent, but this drops to a negative 5 per cent if the consumer can be persuaded to click and collect. Fulfilling from an automated centralized warehouse, which generates a negative margin of 7 per cent, is also more efficient than store fulfilment in their calculations.

Some retailers experiment by offering pickup discounts to click-and-collect online shoppers or increasing prices for some items purchased online. For example, in 2017, at Walmart, a bag of tortilla chips sold for $3.83 if delivered, but only $1.74 if picked up at the store.[14] After consumers complained about the differential pricing, Walmart began displaying on its website both the lower in-store as well as the higher online prices if delivered to the home. Since 2020, it has matched prices for the same products, irrespective of the channel. Unfortunately, from a retail economics perspective, this sets the wrong incentives for shoppers.

For the last-mile delivery, the two favoured models are ship-from-store and ship-from-warehouse. While retailers with extensive physical store networks usually rely on ship-from-store and in-store picking by employing additional staff, Amazon has invested in developing shipping from the warehouse and automated dark store picking.[15] The contrast between ship-from-store, as Walmart does, versus ship-from-warehouse, as Amazon prefers, is the focus of the next chapter.

For Walmart to pursue delivery of online grocery sales or online sales of anything, in general, is clashing with Amazon in the latter's home field. Amazon has built an infrastructure to deliver online orders as fast, accurately and efficiently as possible. Walmart, like other incumbent physical store retailers, is caught between a rock and a hard place, unable to ignore consumer demands for an omnichannel experience and unable to deliver orders profitably. And if their view is that ultimately, it will be impossible to avoid a head-on clash with Amazon, then they need to aggressively push both marketplace and retail media or advertising.

Advertising to the Rescue

All this financial analysis demonstrating the impossibility of achieving profitability in online retailing for Amazon begs the obvious question: Why then is Amazon scaling up so rapidly? The highly lucrative advertising business for Amazon is only possible because of the data they have on past purchases. Amazon has, over the past few years, overtaken Google in the US as the engine on which people start their search for products. In a survey in June 2019, when US Internet users aged thirteen and older were asked where they 'typically start' when shopping for a product online, 49 per cent said they went to Amazon versus 22 per cent for Google.[16] In addition, among those who normally shopped online or were Amazon Prime members, the number of those who started on Amazon was much higher.

Of course, the advertising business for Amazon depends heavily on Marketplace. The point is that Prime, Marketplace and advertising have a mutually reinforcing relationship with each other that exists on top of, and because of, Amazon's own online retail sales. However, competitors like Walmart must confront the question: Do we have a data monetization strategy to cover the losses and an AWS-type business to subsidize the ramping up of operations? As the answer to the AWS-type business is likely to be no, physical retailers must develop retail media (advertising) and marketplace ecosystems as well as encourage click-and-collect in their clash with Amazon. The fact that Walmart is larger than Amazon in online grocery sales in the US suggests that this strategy is working to some extent for Walmart in its battle with Amazon. Retail media will be addressed in greater detail in the final chapter, but following Amazon's success with advertising, large retailers are evolving into media companies.

In conclusion, just like Google provides search 'free' to netizens in return for selling searchers' eyeballs to advertisers, and Facebook provides social networking 'free' in return for selling user demographic data and 'likes' to brands, Amazon is providing retailing 'free' in return for selling shoppers' past purchase data to marketplace vendors. If you are getting the service for free, then you are the product being sold!

Chapter Takeaways

- At first glance, online retailing appears to require fewer assets (store real estate, inventory) and lower operating expenses (staff, merchandising) relative to brick-and-mortar stores. But online retail replaces consumer labour (visit to the store) with retailer labour (fulfilment to home).
- Amazon Prime has mistakenly led consumers to believe that delivery should be 'free' and shoppers are unable to accurately comprehend the costs to retailers of fulfilment.
- Delivery costs at Amazon as a percentage of online retail sales demonstrated some improvement over the years preceding the introduction of Prime (2002–2007) from 24 per cent to 17 per cent.
- With the introduction of Prime, Amazon shoppers have no incentive to be efficient in their ordering (bundle items

for larger orders). As the number of Prime subscribers has increased over the years, delivery cost as a percentage of online retail sales has steadily deteriorated.

- For 2022, Amazon is devoting more than 40 cents of every online retail dollar to delivery. Assuming a minimum of another 10 per cent in operating costs, they are running retail at a negative 25 per cent (assuming a gross margin of 25 per cent) margin. Online retailing at Amazon is a loss leader, subsidized by Marketplace, advertising and AWS.

- Surprisingly, if one compares Amazon retail operations to Walmart, Walmart achieves higher asset and inventory turnover ratios! Even sales per employee are similar for the two firms.

- Online retail can be a profitable business if the products are digital, consumers are willing to pay the full delivery costs or the gross margin per order in absolute dollars generated is relatively high compared to delivery costs.

- Grocery delivery is an unprofitable business as the dollars generated per order are too small to cover the complicated (bulky low-margin items, mix of ambient and chilled/frozen items within an order, specific delivery slots) delivery costs.

- As a business model, Amazon is evolving to be closer to Google and Meta. Google gives search, Meta offers social networking and Amazon provides online retail for 'free' in return for selling customer data to advertisers.

6

The Last-Mile Challenge

In the sprawling city of Metropolis, there lived a young woman named Maya. With dreams of pursuing a degree in fine arts, she had eagerly moved here, hoping to find work that would support her education and passion. However, the job market proved to be challenging, with opportunities scarce and competition fierce.

In her search for income, Maya stumbled upon the world of the gig economy. The promise of flexible hours, the ability to work from anywhere and the potential to earn seemed like a perfect fit for her situation. She signed up on a platform called 'SwiftShift' where she could offer her skills as a graphic designer to clients seeking quick and affordable designs.

At first, Maya was excited. She received her first gig, a simple logo design for a small local business. She poured her heart into the work, meticulously crafting a design that she felt proud of. The process, however, was more time-consuming than she had anticipated as she had to communicate with the client, make revisions and ensure the design met their expectations.

When she finally submitted her work, she was disheartened to find that the pay was significantly lower than what she had hoped for. After deducting the platform's fees and the time spent on communication and revisions, her hourly wage had dwindled to mere pennies. Despite her efforts, Maya realized that she had been exploited by the gig economy's deceptive allure of flexibility and independence.

Undeterred, Maya continued to take on gigs, hoping that with time, she could build a steady stream of income. However, she soon found herself trapped in a cycle of underpaid work. SwiftShift's competitive pricing structure forced her to lower her rates to attract clients, but the constant stream of revisions and client demands left her with little time to pursue her studies or personal projects.

Maya's health began to deteriorate as the stress of meeting tight deadlines and stretching her meagre earnings took a toll on her well-being. The dream of pursuing her passion in fine arts felt further and further away, replaced by the harsh reality of survival in the gig economy.

One day, while scrolling through social media, Maya stumbled upon a post discussing workers' rights in the gig economy. She learnt about the stories of countless individuals who, like her, had fallen victim to exploitative practices. Inspired by the stories of those who had stood up against injustice, Maya decided to act.

She connected with a local organization advocating for gig workers' rights. Together, they raised awareness about the challenges gig workers faced: the lack of fair compensation, the absence of benefits and the precarious nature of the work. Maya's story became a rallying point, shedding light on the hidden struggles of gig workers who had been enduring exploitation silently.

Maya's courage sparked a movement. Together with others, she advocated for fair wages, transparent pricing structures and basic protections for gig workers. SwiftShift was forced to

re-evaluate its policies, and other gig platforms faced pressure
to address the exploitative practices that had become rampant.
Maya's story highlighted the urgent need to address the darker
side of the gig economy and sparked conversations about the
value of fair compensation and respect for all forms of labour.

The Challenge of Fulfilling Online Orders

Shoppers love the convenience of ordering online. However,
as we observed in the previous chapter, fulfilling online orders
profitably is challenging. The value proposition of online retail
disruptors such as Amazon or Ocado is to deliver punctually,
accurately and at a low cost to the consumer. In addition,
for incumbent brick-and-mortar retailers, the challenge is in
responding to customer demands for omnichannel offerings
while ensuring that online orders are not earnings-dilutive.
Therefore, both types of retailers have no choice but to grapple
with the economic and logistical challenges of last-mile delivery.

Online disruptors and traditional store retailers approach
last-mile delivery from opposite ends. Since pure-play online
retailers have no store footprint, at least initially, they fulfil
orders from large central warehouses that have been purpose-
built. In contrast, incumbent brick-and-mortar retailers, as
they start servicing the few online orders that trickle in, prefer
to fulfil them from the store closest to the online shopper.
Consequently, Walmart primarily practises store picking to
leverage its vast store network while Amazon's model is centred
on the efficiencies generated by warehouse picking.

In this chapter, we compare the warehouse and store
fulfilment strategies with respect to picking, delivery, collection,
returns, scalability, investment and operating costs. Despite the
scale of Amazon and Walmart as the two largest companies in
the world, neither has solved the last-mile delivery challenge in

a cost-efficient manner. Yet, their efforts through experiments and innovations continue and hold important lessons for all retailers pursuing online sales. However, as a deeper look into Amazon will reveal, the investments required for the last mile are enormous. Finally, we delve into more general problems with respect to profits, people and the planet plaguing the exploding gig economy. Is the day of reckoning coming on these fronts?

Fulfilment via Stores versus Warehouses

Table 6.1 lists the differences between warehouse and store fulfilment. Clearly, each has its advantages and drawbacks. The warehouse model enables greater picking efficiency as it deals with a larger number of orders, allows better utilization of pickers and has a layout optimized for the picking process. Instead of single-order picks assigned to an individual, a warehouse allows for more sophisticated models with greater automation and zone picking—the orders and pickers are assigned to a zone.

Consolidated inventory at a warehouse means fewer out-of-stocks, larger assortments and hence, more complete orders in comparison to decentralized store inventory. For groceries, store picking may suffer from 2–5 per cent of the items being substituted or missing entirely from the order. Nothing is more irritating for the online shopper than an incomplete basket because it necessitates a visit to the store, negating the entire rationale for ordering online. However, although warehouse picking may result in fewer errors and higher strike rates, the judgement of human pickers in stores may be superior, particularly when it comes to selecting fresh produce.

Store picking is not as efficient as warehouse picking because a store layout is not optimized for picking but for merchandising, impulse shopping and customer flow to maximize in-store sales.

Table 6.1. Store Versus Warehouse Fulfilment

	Store	Warehouse
Picking	• Human judgement of quality • More out-of-stocks • Customer interference	• Automated • Picking efficiency • Fewer errors • Larger assortment
Delivery	• Shorter routes • Faster delivery times	• Truck optimization • Longer delivery times
Collection	• Can offer click-and-collect	• Cannot offer click-and-collect
Returns	• Returns to store possible	• Need to develop dedicated return process
Scalability	• Can start small • Limited scalability	• Need scale to justify • Greater control over process
Investment	• No capital investment	• Substantial capital
Operating costs	• Higher operating costs	• Lower operating costs at scale

It is impossible to introduce automation at a store that serves the dual purpose of satisfying in-store and online shoppers. Consistent with this, neither Walmart's distribution centres, nor its stores, are designed for optimal fulfilment of online orders. Its distribution centres have been set up with state-of-the-art technology to operate with extreme efficiency, but that is only for bulk movement of the goods to the stores. They are not suitable for deliveries to individual customers. Therefore, while the distribution centre's system can handle the movement of, say, 150 toothbrushes in one go, it cannot service the order of a single toothbrush. Thus, Walmart delivers online orders primarily from its stores.

Typically, pickers are incentivized by the number of items they pick up accurately in a specific amount of time. However, the presence of regular shoppers at a physical store hinders their ability to pick fast. When the number of online orders is low, it is still manageable. Generally, with the decline in offline shopping, the picking capacity per store is found to be around 100–200 orders per day. However, e-commerce now accounts for 14 per cent of Walmart's sales, or $82 billion. The increase in the number of online orders (for delivery or click-and-collect) makes picking in the store along with maintaining the in-store shopper experience a considerable challenge for Walmart. As Nazim Salur, co-founder of the ten-minute delivery service Getir, observed, 'Their (big grocers) main business is customers coming to their stores—when pickers walk into stores, customers are not happy with that. Logically, doing it all from the same store makes sense, but in real life, it doesn't really work.'[1]

Store picking allows the retailer to offer a click-and-collect service—order online and pick up from the store, as an option. Click-and-collect is cheaper for the retailer to fulfil, allows more flexibility to shoppers, though they need to travel to a store, and creates opportunities for impulse sales. Retailers save on shipping costs as click-and-collect orders require no delivery, only picking.

Walmart leverages its existing infrastructure (more than 4700 stores in the US) for click-and-collect. It offers customers the convenience of ordering online and collecting their orders from its brick-and-mortar store located closest to them. Moreover, the pickup towers in front of the stores provide customers with a faster, hassle-free collection experience. However, this convenience to the customers hinders Walmart's ability to cross-sell. Under the click-and-collect model, only if the customer comes into the store would there be opportunities to cross-sell. However, most shoppers prefer to collect their orders from the kerbside or the pickup towers without entering the store.

Store picking can work even if only a few customers order online. It does not require a large number of online orders to be viable, as the stores primarily exist for offline shoppers. In contrast, a warehouse must have adequate volume to justify operations. The warehouse model makes scaling up much faster and easier if the required capital investment is available. Store picking, on the other hand, is not scalable because with too many orders, pickers begin to interfere with the customers shopping at a store, unless picking is done after closing time or at night.

A warehouse model for fulfilment, such as Amazon has, allows for greater optimization of delivery vehicles as the number of orders being fulfilled from a warehouse is much larger than from a store. However, since these massive warehouses are located where land is cheap, they are farther away from major population centres. Therefore, the delivery vehicles must travel far and may have longer delivery times. With store picking, delivery is faster as the order is usually picked from a store closest to the shopper, and stores, by their nature, are in densely populated locations. The stores' location and retail set-ups also allow customers to make returns easily, while the warehouse delivery model must develop a separate, dedicated and more expensive returns process.

The warehouse model, being a centralized system, provides greater control over training, processes and quality than the store model, which requires managing hundreds, if not thousands, of stores. It also has lower picking and delivery costs, especially at full capacity utilization. Nevertheless, observers sometimes underestimate the high capital investment needed in building warehouse facilities with automation and staffing costs, as we will see later in the chapter when discussing Amazon's last-mile challenges. While the store model usually has higher fulfilment (picking and delivery) costs relative to the warehouse model, unless a large percentage of shoppers select click-and-collect, fulfilment from the stores requires minimal (e.g., collection towers) additional capital investment by traditional offline retailers.

Confronting Last-Mile Challenges at Walmart

We discussed in the previous chapter that for Walmart and other traditional retailers, fulfilling online orders is earnings-dilutive. Click-and-collect orders incur the additional cost of picking while click-and-deliver orders run up costs of delivery as well. With customers expecting uniform pricing across both offline and online channels, the profitability for brick-and-mortar retailers of online orders will inevitably be lower compared to when customers buy at their stores. Any delivery fees charged for online orders do not fully cover fulfilment costs for the retailer on relatively low value products.

Among the online orders, click-and-collect ones tend to be more profitable (or more precisely, less loss-making) for the retailer than those that require home delivery. As mentioned in the previous chapter, while the average negative margin is 5 per cent for the click-and-collect ones versus -15 per cent for delivery-to-home orders, customers, as is to be expected, are reluctant to pay a 'delivery' fee for click-and-collect orders. This shrinks the 'after delivery fees' profitability between click-and-collect versus home delivery orders, even if home delivery orders are still relatively more unprofitable.

Realizing that online orders are not going to be profitable, supermarkets in the US have been generally unenthusiastic about them. This has led to the emergence of services like Instacart, which targets existing grocery retailers. A gig economy model, like Uber, Instacart hires freelance shoppers to pick customers' orders from nearby grocery stores and deliver the orders to their homes. The retailer does not need to invest in any dedicated staff or logistical facilities to serve the online shopper but has to pay a fee per order to Instacart. On such online orders, the retailer does not incur any picking and shipping costs, nor does it collect any delivery fees. Shoppers pay Instacart directly for the service through an annual subscription and a per-order fee. While not as unprofitable as home delivery, these orders via Instacart will still be less profitable for the retailer than shoppers coming into the store, because the retailer has to share its margin with Instacart. As we observed in the case of Amazon, it is only the data collected by Amazon and the resulting advertising revenues that make its retail business of online order fulfilment of mass products worthwhile. The big problem for retailers using Instacart for their online orders is that they are effectively handing over all the data to Instacart.

To compensate for the loss of earnings in online orders, Walmart has used its access to customers to attract online merchants. Since 2016, by adding marketplace capabilities, the retailer has increased its inventory manifold, offering more than 170 million products from over 1,00,000 online sellers. This helps Walmart improve its online value proposition versus Amazon with respect to assortment. Furthermore, marketplace orders are profitable for Walmart as the vendors manage the delivery or pay Walmart to do so. Thus, Walmart is monetizing its customer base by collecting commissions on third-party vendor sales. This also enables the retailer to build an advertising business model similar to Amazon, even if it is relatively small for now (estimated at a tenth of Amazon). Yet, the growth of online retailing has led to increased investments in support of e-commerce for Walmart. The earnings-dilutive effects of e-commerce for Walmart over the past decade can be observed in its lower absolute dollar net income, operating margins, return on assets and return on equity (see Table 2.1).

Confronting Last-Mile Challenges at Amazon

We saw in the previous chapter, a large portion of Amazon's sales dollar goes into fulfilment costs. Amazon's retail profitability, both operating margins and return on investment, is highly dependent on its last-mile performance. The retailer's ability to grow and drive its share further, especially in grocery and apparel, is contingent upon the extent of control and efficiency it has over the last mile of connectivity with its customers.

Consequently, Amazon is pouring considerable effort and investment into solving the last-mile challenge. It has been continuously experimenting with and developing innovative solutions for pickup, delivery and return of items. This includes establishing a physical footprint in the domain through strategic acquisitions and partnerships with other players. Furthermore, these investments in last-mile delivery enrich Amazon data and asset flywheels, which increasingly drives the growth of 'non-retail' revenues.

Encouraging Click-and-Collect

While warehouses cannot offer click-and-collect to reduce fulfilment costs since they are neither located nor set up for customer visits, Amazon is encouraging customers to click-and-collect from Amazon counters. This allows customers to order from Amazon and then pick up their order from a designated physical location, usually a mom-and-pop store, convenience store or pharmacy. This reduces shipping costs for Amazon as in one trip, it can now deliver, let us say, ten different orders to a single counter location instead of ten separate drop-offs to ten different addresses. Some customers also prefer click-and-collect as they may be in the area in any case and do not want to wait at home to receive deliveries as otherwise, they would have to, especially for groceries.

More than 2000 self-service delivery locations for pickup and return have been opened across fifty-plus major metropolitan areas in the US, including select Whole Foods stores. Unfortunately, there is little incentive for Amazon Prime customers, who comprise most of Amazon's sales volume, to click-and-collect when deliveries-to-home are 'free'. Thus, it is difficult to see any substantial beneficial impact of the click-and-collect service on Amazon's shipping costs.

Experimenting with Physical Stores

The 2017 Amazon acquisition of Whole Foods added grocery capabilities. Ownership of over 400 grocery stores enabled Amazon to offer click-and-collect services for the groceries bought from Whole Foods, enjoy a higher operating margin (5 per cent), provide the 'touch and feel' grocery experience and offer these locations as points of delivery for other online orders. It also allowed the retailer to tap into the quality-conscious customer base of Whole Foods, which is similar to its Prime members—those who are willing to pay more for quality and convenience.

Besides the Whole Foods acquisition, Amazon has experimented with several other physical store formats, all rather unsuccessfully. It opened a bookstore in 2015 and expanded to more than twenty such formats in the US before announcing in 2022 that they will be shut down. In 2016, it established Amazon Go, a futuristic convenience store with no cashiers and checkouts. While there were rumours that it planned to open 2000 such stores, in 2023, Amazon announced the closure of eight Amazon Go stores in major cities like New York and San Francisco. In 2020, the retailer launched

Amazon Fresh, its first brick-and-mortar supermarket, and has expanded it to twenty-nine stores in the US and fifteen in the UK. But once again, at the end of 2022, Amazon announced they were pausing expansion pending evaluation. The retailer had also established eighty-seven pop-up stores and miniature retail storefronts (300 to 500 square feet) in the middle of shopping malls to carry an assortment of Amazon hardware devices. However, these were discontinued in 2022. Finally, treasure trucks, another much-heralded Amazon experiment, also seem to have been phased out.

Recall from our earlier chapters that Walmart has built a business model perfected for physical stores and for Amazon to compete with that would require a completely different set of capabilities. And, in any case, it dominates the value proposition of convenience and delivery to home. Venturing out of that 'sweet spot' only turns its core competencies into core rigidities, which stops the retailer from changing and competing effectively. Amazon seems to be better off focusing on improving the home fulfilment engine.

Improving the Delivery Experience

In 2011, Amazon introduced a locker system, installing self-service kiosks in public places such as retail stores and office buildings in large US cities for pickup or return of packages at a time and place convenient to shoppers. Later, in 2017, the retailer extended this service by launching the hub locker delivery system for apartment blocks and other housing complexes so that residents could receive and pick up packages at flexible times. This 24/7 service obliterated the need for the shopper to be at home at the time of delivery, or the need for the presence of a doorman or a concierge, hence offering the shopper more convenience while allowing the retailer a certain amount of control over the logistics of the last-mile delivery.

When the company first rolled out Amazon Lockers, some early observers pointed out that the programme could help cut down shipping costs. 'Users don't pay extra to use the service but the locker programme helps Amazon save on certain shipping costs,' the *Wall Street Journal* optimistically wrote back in 2012.[2] A decade after it launched, there are now 2800 Amazon Lockers throughout the US, but shipping costs are as high as ever. Customers often complain about the lockers being full due to the high volume of deliveries.[3]

Amazon Key is yet another innovative service offered by the retailer, which enables Prime members to receive and view the delivery being made inside their front door when they are not at home. However, to do so, customers need to buy a compatible smart lock and a security camera specially made for the programme. According to Rohit Shrivastava, general manager of Amazon Key, the customer benefits of the service extend beyond it being a delivery mechanism, 'It's a great service for busy families; you no longer have to worry about giving keys to service providers like house cleaners, instead, you can give them their own code right from your Amazon Key App.'[4]

The company has also rolled out Amazon's 'Key for Business' service that requires building complexes to install a device on the front door, which will allow delivery drivers to get into the lobby at all hours without having to be buzzed inside.[5] This has made deliveries faster and reduced theft.

Amazon also introduced the concept of Prime Air, a delivery service using drones (unmanned aerial vehicles) in 2013. While unfavourable Federal Aviation Administration (FAA) regulations had earlier limited this initiative in the US, in 2020, the FAA designated Amazon Prime Air as an 'air carrier', allowing it to begin commercial deliveries under a trial programme.[6] It is doubtful that drone delivery is going to be big except in remote areas. Imagine thousands of drones filling the skies trying to deliver packages in New York City every minute. It would be chaos!

Bringing Logistics In-House

To reduce its dependence on third parties such as UPS, FedEx and USPS for deliveries, in 2014, Amazon started building its global transportation network. While they do not reveal the capital specifically employed towards this initiative, it is interesting to note that capital expenditure in 2022 was $64 billion compared to $3.4 billion in 2013—an increase of almost twenty times in ten years. Of course, revenues have also increased during this period, but capital expenditures are at 12–13 per cent of revenues compared to 4–5 per cent in 2013. Why does logistics require such high capital spending and what are the benefits of in-house delivery for Amazon?

Investments in delivery infrastructure include land, warehouses, sorting centres, delivery stations and vehicles. Despite Bezos's initial aversion to buying property, Amazon has emerged with a large real estate portfolio. Most retailers own their land and stores, as this gives them greater control than leases and allows participation in the upside when these assets appreciate. In addition, over time, Amazon warehouses have become highly specialized in character and can cost twice as much to build as a standard warehouse. This limits the number of developers willing to custom-build and lease to Amazon at a cost-efficient rate. As a result, Amazon has been buying large tracts of land to build warehouses or acquiring properties for redevelopment. For instance, it bought 63 acres for $30 million in Southern California to build a 40-metre-tall state-of-the-art warehouse.[7] During the pandemic years of 2020 and 2021, the unexpected surge in demand led Amazon to open one logistics facility a day! Realizing that it overbuilt then, it has now slowed down considerably.

Over and above the large warehouses quintessentially identified with Amazon, it has built smaller sorting centres that work with the US Postal Service (USPS) and delivery stations where the orders are loaded on to vans for last-mile delivery. In 2022, Amazon had 1285 distribution centres of various types in the US, with 305 large fulfilment centres, 207 sorting centres and 656 delivery stations, which exceeded 400 million square feet of space.[8]

Amazon has also invested in building a $1.5 billion air cargo hub to deliver items from third-party sellers directly to customers, bypassing the traditional cargo carriers.[9] After four years of planning and construction, the 8,00,000 square feet hub opened in August 2021, with plans to connect a network of forty sites, operate a dozen flights per day and process millions of packages every week.[10]

To fully comprehend the capital needs of this delivery infrastructure, combine all the above with 40,000 semi-trucks, 30,000 vans and over seventy planes. Besides, there are huge operating costs of running this system, which requires 4,00,000 drivers worldwide.[11] This investment is still nowhere close to being complete as Amazon has, for example, on order, 1,00,000 electric vans. The last-mile fulfilment network is capital-hungry and most competitors will be unable to fund such large investments. Moreover, the Amazon strategy to build this last-mile capability is simplified here to make exposition easy. In reality, Amazon, as Table 6.2 demonstrates, has a complex web of acquisitions (buy), partnerships and strategic investments (borrow) to complement and further its in-house (build) fulfilment capabilities. There is also a massive hiring spree to run the network; the Amazon workforce is now more

Table 6.2. Amazon's Build, Buy and Borrow Fulfilment Strategy

		Investment	Acquisition	Partnership
Freight & Logistics	Air Cargo	• ATSG • CargoJet	• Canvas	
	Autonomous Logistics	• Aurora • Plus		
	Grocery & Food Delivery	• Deliveroo • SpartanNash		• Morrisons
	Zero-Emissions Logistics	• Beta • Infinium • ION Energy • Lion Electric • Redwood Materials • Resilient Power • Rivian • Turntide		• eo • Mahindra Electric
Connected vehicle tech				• ABB • Blackberry QNX • BMW • Elektrobit • Ford • Netradyne • Nvidia • Toyota
In-vehicle infotainment				• Audi • BMW • FCA • Ford • Garmin • GM • Hyundai • Lucid • Nissan • Telenav • Voxx Automotive
Mobility as a service		• Shuttl	• Zoox	• Uber

Source: Adapted from CB Insights; since 2019, not an exhaustive list of Amazon's activities

than 1.5 million-strong. So much for the initial story of the asset- and people-light online business model!

The last-mile build, buy and borrow capabilities strategy is generating many benefits for Amazon which, arguably, is erecting the world's largest competitive moat for the retailer. First, it is estimated that there is a $2–4 per package decline in cost per package when delivered via Amazon versus using external shippers. Amazon is now shipping 72 per cent of its own packages versus close to 20 per cent in early 2018. Having exited the FedEx relationship some time ago, the retailer has also reduced its dependence on UPS and USPS. While it is hard to get the actual numbers, in 2021, it is estimated that Amazon delivered 5 billion packages in the US versus 5.5 billion by UPS. Currently, it is widely assumed that Amazon is larger than UPS in the number of packages delivered. It has become a logistics behemoth.

Second, this investment has enabled the retailer to offer logistics as a service. 'Fulfilled by Amazon' (FBA) allows Amazon to charge third-party sellers on its own site for delivering products on the sellers' behalf. More recently, Amazon has even started offering this service to others who are not selling via the Amazon website. In this sense, it is following the AWS business that Amazon built so successfully, which started by selling to others the excess server capacity that Amazon did not require.

Asset and Data Flywheels

Most important are the less visible benefits of building mutually reinforcing flywheels on assets and data.[12] The asset flywheel is what allows Amazon to offer logistics as a service to third parties. Manufacturers and suppliers can move to leaner operations by simply plugging into Amazon's logistics and delivery infrastructure. For many suppliers, given their small volumes and the capital-intensive nature of the last-mile delivery, it makes sense to use Amazon's end-to-end delivery service. This lowers the delivery cost for everyone, including Amazon, while enabling Amazon's logistics operations to achieve economies of scale and scope.

The enormous data generated by the added infrastructure feeds Amazon's continuously improving prediction model. It runs routes (e.g., integrating driver, weather, traffic data), fleet (e.g., integrating vehicle, package sizes and weights, destination data) and delivery (e.g., integrating time of delivery, parking facilities at destination, access such as deliver to mailroom, reception, front door). The more data generated by the system, the better the models perform to deliver packages more accurately, punctually and cost-efficiently.

Suppliers who utilize Amazon logistics can also benefit from the data flywheel. Amazon develops deep customer insights, which can be provided for targeting, recommendation, manufacturing and stocking purposes to suppliers. By observing which products are being ordered by which localities, Amazon's shipping model can anticipate demand to delight customers and improve the utilization of the infrastructure. For example, knowing that a certain number of iPhone 14s are being ordered daily in a particular neighbourhood, Amazon can ship them in advance to a delivery centre close by, ensuring delivery in four hours instead of the next day. It also helps stock optimization since it reduces inventory and out-of-stocks simultaneously.

The greater the scale, the more data is generated and the more valuable insights deduced for sale to the larger Amazon network. Besides the revenue enhancements, this improves Amazon's own cost performance. The Amazon prediction models keep getting better with increasing scale and usage. While late to the game relative to Google and Microsoft with investments in building AI capability, Amazon's data can deliver tremendous benefits when combined with generative AI. The learning models will simply get better and help increase revenues and service levels while delivering cost efficiencies.

Profits, People and Planet Dilemmas of Delivery

With the rise of the gig economy, the boundaries between online industries are blurring. The gig economy, also referred to as the sharing economy, consists of independent contractors, who provide services such as ride share and delivery of online orders (e.g., food, grocery). Instacart, Uber, Grab and Just Eat are examples of firms that have tied up with retailers and restaurants to offer delivery of online purchases. The mushrooming of such firms in response to online consumer demand has led to many people being employed by the gig economy worldwide. This has brought into greater scrutiny the employment practices of such firms. In addition, the environmental footprint of these delivery services and their inherent profitability need to be considered as well. These business models face dilemmas regarding profits, people and the planet.

Profits

The worldwide gig economy is populated by a large set of firms. For the purposes of this book, our interest is only in those companies that provide last-mile services for everyday products and not firms such as Airbnb, TaskRabbit or Upwork, which are pure platforms. Table 6.3 presents some of the largest gig economy platforms that are heavily involved in delivering online orders from retailers and restaurants as well as ride-sharing. These include Deliveroo (UK), DoorDash, Grab (Singapore, Southeast Asia), Instacart, Lyft, Swiggy (India), Uber and Zomato (India).

Table 6.3. Delivery Firms in Billions

Name	Revenues	Income
Deliveroo	£1.97	£-0.24
DoorDash	$6.58	$-1.37
Grab	$1.43	$-1.74
Instacart (privately held)	$2.50	$0.43
Lyft	$4.10	$-1.60
Swiggy	Rs 57.0	Rs -36.3
Uber	$31.88	-9.14 $
Zomato	Rs 86.9	Rs -7.8
Just Eat	€5.56	€-5.77

1. All numbers for calendar year 2022, except Zomato for year ending March 2023.
2. Just Eat had impairments from acquisitions. Ignoring those losses of €792 million.

We know from our analysis that Amazon's core online retail business is not profitable on account of the delivery costs, so it is not surprising that all these delivery apps also struggle with profitability (see Table 6.3). The exception, Instacart, in 2022, was because it was being dressed up for an IPO in 2023. In 2022, shoppers spent $29 billion on Instacart, which resulted in $2.5 billion in revenues for the company. Advertising at $740 million accounted for 30 per cent of this revenue. Of the $428 million profits it reported, $358 million came from what Instacart described as a 'tax benefit'! While popular with customers (who does not love subsidized services?), Instacart is barely profitable as a business model. Given the delivery app's limited scope of cross-selling opportunities (relative to an Amazon which sells everything), it is harder for Instacart's advertising to compensate for the core delivery losses. No wonder, its market cap in November 2023 was around $7 billion, a far cry from the $39 billion in 2021, when it was hyped because of COVID-19.

A cautionary note on the sustainability of the Instacart business model comes from China. Enamoured by Instacart, start-ups rushed into the home delivery app space. However, more than 150 Chinese grocery delivery start-ups have failed over the years, and this is despite the much lower wage rates in China relative to the US or Europe. It is almost impossible to make money as customers are price-sensitive, delivery staff switch jobs for pennies, entry barriers are low and the dollar margins per order are small.

Unlike Amazon, which customers rate as high on customer satisfaction and value, the firms listed in Table 6.3, despite their unprofitable operations, are often criticized for charging too much by those they partner with (e.g., restaurants, retailers), paying too little to those they employ (the freelance gig workforce) and charging the end consumers too much. Restaurants complain that they lose money on online orders because of the discovery and delivery charges levied as well as the discounts forced by the apps. These may total as high as 30 per cent of sales for a restaurant, and then there are the extra packaging costs. The press is full of stories on the exploitation of gig workers on account of long working hours, few benefits and poor hourly wages. Yet, Uber pronounced in its third-quarter earnings release, 'cumulative payments to drivers for . . . deliveries . . . historically exceeded the cumulative delivery fees paid by consumer.'[13] And finally, consumers feel extorted because of 'surge pricing' and have pushed for regulations in some countries to limit it. However, over time, as with the airline dynamic pricing models, consumers do get accustomed to, and increasingly accept, surge pricing.

The fundamental problem with these business models is the lack of differentiation, which gives the platforms no pricing power. Everyone engages in 'multi-homing'—users joining more than one platform. As a consumer, you have multiple apps and you check prices on each before ordering, thus limiting what an app can charge as delivery fees. On the supplier side, any increase in commission leads the restaurant to switch providers. Ride-sharing drivers often list themselves with two different apps (e.g., Uber and Lyft in the USA, Grab and Gojek in Singapore, and Uber and Ola in India) and opt for the more lucrative option to pick up riders. The only saving grace for these apps is the duopoly structure (two major players) in most markets does allow some protection from price competition.

Amazon compensates by generating profits through its customer data, but for these apps, the customer data play has presented a big challenge. They are in a fight with retailers and restaurants on who owns the data generated. In 2021, the New York City Council passed legislation that required apps to share customer data (names, phone numbers, email and delivery addresses) with restaurants unless a customer opted out.[14] A lawsuit by DoorDash and UberEats led the city to back off. However, with the increasing popularity of these apps, the fights on who owns the data, on workforce protection and on surge pricing will increasingly move to regulators, legislators and courts.

In its current incarnation, this is a challenged business model, despite Instacart finally generating significant advertising revenues. Brands do see it as a platform for advertising to shoppers. However, it is harder to imagine substantial advertising revenues for ride-sharing and food delivery apps as the pool of advertisers and conversion rates will be smaller relative to Amazon, Instacart or Walmart, where you can seamlessly purchase the advertised product. While taking a ride or ordering your meal, the cross-selling opportunities are limited. You are not looking for another meal or ride, nor anything else to buy. The most recent results are not encouraging for delivery apps across the world. In 2023, Zomato closed operations in

225 cities, Deliveroo pulled out of Australia, DoorDash cut
6 per cent of its corporate headcount or 1250 employees, and
Grubhub, owned by Just Eat, laid off 2800 workers or 15 per
cent of its workforce.

Yes, consumers love them, growth is spectacular, but profits
are absent. Moreover, given our analysis of the effects of scale
in the case of Amazon, there is no easy path to profitability for
these apps if delivery is where they hope to make money.

People

It is estimated that there are over 1.1 billion on-demand gig
workers worldwide.[15] Uber, like other firms in this sector,
argues that their workforce is self-employed and hence does
not qualify for pensions, healthcare benefits, vacation days,
sick leave or protection from dismissal. Moreover, there should
be no limits on hours worked per day or days worked per week
as these independent contractors are free to choose. As a result,
there are few employment protections offered to gig workers.
This is unfortunate, as the gig workforce tends to be largely
the most vulnerable sections of the population, although there
are some who opt for gig economy work because they prize the
independence and flexibility it offers.

Before cars were introduced, there were no traffic laws.
Interestingly, it was as late as 1954 when South Dakota
became the last state to mandate drivers' licenses. Similarly,
the law related to the gig economy is evolving. The UK Court
of Appeal ruled that gig workers should be offered the same
protections and benefits as full-time employees, though this
was reversed by the UK Supreme Court.[16] California passed
a law with similar implications, but it has also been appealed
against by the gig economy companies.[17] Since July 2023,
it has been mandatory for app-based delivery workers in

New York to be paid a minimum hourly wage of $17.96, not including tips.

The European Union has been more aggressive in protecting gig workers. Spain amended its laws in 2022 to give gig economy workers similar rights that include collective bargaining. Spain's labour ministry fined Glovo, an app-based food delivery company, €79 million in 2022 and €56.7 million in 2023 for not contracting its riders as employees and for giving gigs to irregular immigrants without work permits.[18] Germany went even further and as a result, some firms like Delivery Hero withdrew from the country in 2021. The company's CEO and co-founder, Niklas Östberg, said that current German labour laws makes it difficult for platforms to hire riders.[19] Anabel Diaz, head of Uber's mobility division in Europe, warned that proposals to designate gig workers as de facto employees would force it to cease operating in hundreds of cities across the EU, and raise prices by as much as 40 per cent in those that it continues to serve.

The technical argument by the gig economy firms for exemption from labour laws is that as a platform, they are merely linking consumers with entrepreneurs. The economic argument is that it is not financially viable for them to treat their gig workers as full-time employed staff. Effectively, this implies that there is a problem with the business model of gig economy firms, with customers unwilling to pay the true cost of delivery. Put another way, these workers, who can ill afford it, are subsidizing the more affluent customers.

A study of gig economy workers in India revealed the rather depressing situation in the country from a people perspective. Somewhere between 7,00,000 to 1 million are deployed by food delivery platforms like Swiggy and Zomato. The nominal income of a food delivery gig worker was 20,026 rupees (less than $300) a month. Unfortunately, the rising cost of fuel and cost of living had led to an 11 per cent decline in real wages for these gig workers between 2019 and 2022. Indicative of the dire employment situation in India, a third of them were holding college degrees![20] Beyond the economic costs, interviews conducted by my MBA students of these gig workers found that the biggest complaint was job-induced stress and health risks. The pressure to meet unrealistic delivery time targets in congested Indian cities increases accident risk and negative ratings for factors beyond their control.

The larger point here is that as a greater number of people are employed in the gig economy, there will be increasing pressure on regulators, courts and legislators to offer adequate protection to this workforce. So far, these platforms have had a relatively free ride, employing vast numbers of people at low costs; yet, the app firms are not profitable. However, things are going to get worse for them as society and governments are increasingly confronted with the ugly side of the gig economy. Compared to, say, a waiter at a restaurant, the app-based worker must navigate restaurant delays, congested traffic, climbing up staircases, unsafe neighbourhoods, barking dogs, spilt food and impatient customers. All this while under the pressures of meeting delivery timelines, constant evaluation via customer ratings, costs of maintaining the vehicle and unpredictable earnings. In addition, there is the fear that mistakes in delivery or customer complaints can quickly result in being barred from the app. There is a clear need to protect gig workers as users are blissfully unaware of these stresses.

Furthermore, unionization efforts are growing, which will inevitably increase costs and reduce the flexibility that these platforms have enjoyed so far. In 2023, 300 employees walked out of Amazon's Coventry warehouse in the UK because of the 'derisory' 5 per cent pay increase to £10.50 (about $13.15) an hour. They also objected to the constant monitoring, especially of idle time. The union alleged that even a trip to the toilet could lead to questions by managers. More provocatively, one employee quipped that at Amazon, the robots 'are treated better than us'.[21] Meanwhile, in the US, more than half the workers at Amazon's Staten Island facility voted to join the labour union, demonstrating the inevitability of some unionization. Much of the efficiency drive of Amazon comes from their performance monitoring system. To defend itself, Amazon argued that they reward great performance and coach those unable to meet it.

With unemployment falling in the US and many app-based firms competing for gig workers, Dara Khosrowshahi, CEO of Uber, himself got behind the wheel to experience a driver's life. In April 2021, Uber put aside $250 million for bonuses to attract drivers. However, the detrimental effect on the financial results led to complaints by investors that he was spending too much. As he noted: 'Historically, we've always put a premium on the rider experience' but we need to also win the 'hearts and minds' of drivers.[22] Despite the profitability pressures on these firms, they will need to confront the 'people' issue, especially in tight labour markets.

Planet

Ride-sharing and delivery apps have led to a much higher number of vehicles, although smaller ones, on busy urban roads. This has increased congestion and reduced available space on kerbsides. In addition, because of ride-sharing services, the use of public transportation has come down, resulting in detrimental effects such as higher carbon emissions and a rise in public transportation fares. Higher fares further increase the incentive to use ride-sharing services instead of public transit. Although, with the increasing use of bicycles and electric vehicles (assuming the electricity is green), the negative impact on the air quality from the home delivery and ride-sharing industry is somewhat reduced. However, it still puts greater pressure on the environment relative to mass transit alternatives.

While these platforms do attempt to encourage multi-drop rides, customer preferences and logistical challenges put a dampener on their adoption. Not too many riders choose to share a ride with others. Similarly, the need to ensure that the food gets delivered quickly to the customer, while it is hot, makes coordination of multiple deliveries on a single trip difficult, and even more so if couriers are working on multiple platforms. Under pressure to meet exacting standards, fatigued gig workers are more likely to violate traffic regulations. Accidents happen as riders attempt to monitor their apps while operating their vehicles. Unfortunately, the current routing algorithms of platforms do not factor in such sustainability concerns.

Anyone who has had food delivered is aware of the 'plastics problem'. Non-sustainable packaging in food delivery is now a significant contributor to environmental waste. The most frequent packaging materials are single-use plastics, which are not biodegradable or made of Styrofoam that takes something like 500 years to decompose. A recent survey estimates that an average of 2.8 food deliveries each week amounts to nearly 1341 plastic items per person each year, generating 10.8 kg of plastic waste.[23] This accounts for 12.2 per cent of an individual's yearly plastic consumption of 88 kg. Most (55 per cent) of plastic packaging in food deliveries is not recyclable, and even if it is, how motivated are consumers to recycle it?[24] One would be surprised if even 10 per cent of the plastic packaging generated by food deliveries was recycled.

Sustainability-focused shoppers, especially in countries that mandate retailers charge for plastic bags, choose to bring their own bags to pack their groceries. However, with online ordering, this choice is not available. At best, you can return bags to online retailers, such as Ocado, on the next delivery for credit. A survey by Zomato indicated that customers do feel guilty about this waste *and over* 90 per cent said that they did not really need the plastic cutlery with their orders. As a result, Zomato made changes and included cutlery as an 'opt-in' instead of the previous 'opt-out' option. Given the scale of Zomato in India, the company estimated that this change will save 5000 kg of plastic daily, amounting to 2 million kg of plastic in a year.[25]

Unlike the plastics problem, or even the congestion caused, which are visible, some of the deleterious effects on the planet from 'delivery' are invisible. End users have no idea what is the environmental footprint of this 'convenience' they have become addicted to. Of course, we know that any product bought has made a lengthy journey with substantial greenhouse gas emissions from the combination of sea, air and road vehicles utilized for this. Returns create a greater negative impact because only half of them are placed on shelves for resale. It was estimated that in the US in 2022, nearly 10 billion pounds of this returned merchandise ended up in landfills. Between 2019 and 2022, carbon dioxide emissions in the US grew by 15 per cent to 24 million metric tons, equivalent to having an additional 5.3 million cars on the roads.

The Dilemma

Unfortunately, Amazon has led the way for online retailing businesses to engage in practices such as free delivery and easy costless returns, setting up perverse incentives for customers. Because of Amazon Prime, customers place multiple small orders and prefer home delivery, rather than bundle multiple items into a single order and opt for at least click-and-collect. Moreover, customers tend to order more items than they need as they know that the unwanted items can be freely returned later from the comfort of their home. Understandably, customers love the convenience of online ordering, but they do not perceive the consequent costs that the system levies on retailers, employees and the environment. The business model pioneered by Amazon, which others are now forced to adopt because of well-formed customer expectations, is unsustainable for the most part from the profit, people and planet perspectives.

Traditional incumbent retailers had been hoping that time would allow them to find an online model that was not earnings-dilutive. Unfortunately, the pandemic forced their hand as online orders skyrocketed. Retailers had to replace profitable store sales with unprofitable online orders. Dave Lewis, the previous CEO of the UK market leader Tesco, acknowledged that online operations did not break even in the past. However, he continues to hope that there is an 'opportunity to be more commercially oriented in the way that we put delivery prices together . . . Do I see a situation into the future where pricing becomes more rational? Yes.' However, hope is not a strategy!

Nearly three-quarters of the top 1000 retailers in the US offer some form of free shipping (usually with a minimum order size) on select orders. Reducing shipping costs is the number one priority for retailers. Unlike Amazon, most of them do not have the luxury of AWS profits, advertising revenues, marketplace commissions or even investor patience. Even Amazon is slowly making changes. Besides increasing the cost of Prime membership, recently, Amazon has restricted its same-day delivery service to only orders above $25. Smaller orders will attract a delivery fee of $2.99. In March 2023, Amazon USA increased the minimum order size for free delivery of Prime grocery shopping from $35 to $150. Orders below that level have to pay an additional delivery charge of between $3.95 and

$9.95. While shoppers may be addicted to free shipping, online retailers will have to start weaning them away.

Over the next decade, the fundamental question for physical store retailers, who wish to avoid the spate of bankruptcies that have struck this sector, is to find a proposition to coexist alongside e-commerce. It is to this we turn in the next chapter: How can physical stores survive and thrive in the evolving digital retail landscape? What can they offer to consumers as a compelling proposition to draw them to the brick-and-mortar store? These questions are relevant not only to the clash between Amazon and Walmart but to any physical store chain.

Chapter Takeaways

- Relative to warehouse picking, store picking has the advantage of shorter delivery routes, faster delivery times as well as the ability to offer click-and-collect and returns to the store. Brick-and-mortar retailers prefer store fulfilment as it requires no additional capital investment.
- Relative to store picking, warehouse picking enables automation and picking efficiency, and results in fewer errors and out-of-stocks. Pure play online retailers prefer warehouse shipping as it optimizes fulfilment cost, even if it requires heavy capital investment.
- Despite online sales being earnings-dilutive, Walmart, like other brick-and-mortar retailers, is forced to offer them. Following Amazon's lead, it is expanding into marketplace and advertising.
- Amazon's initiatives to reduce shipping costs have run into obstacles: click-and-collect (no incentive for Prime customers), its physical stores (not a growth business), Amazon lockers in apartment buildings (complaints about being always full), Amazon Key (customer reluctance to

allow home access) and Amazon Air (obtaining approval for drone delivery).

- The scale at which Amazon now fulfils orders has forced it to move logistics in-house. But capital investment and staffing costs have ballooned in the push to provide faster delivery through a hub and spoke model of large fulfilment centres, regional sortation centres and local delivery stations. Amazon is now generating revenues from this capability by offering logistics as a service business to any online retailer.

- Despite being unprofitable, app-based gig economy firms face pushback from businesses and customers for overcharging and from employees for poor wages. With no competitive differentiation and customers who are unappreciative of the cost of delivery, it appears to be a flawed business model. Users may be addicted to free delivery, but change is necessary.

7

Strategies for Brick-and-Mortar Stores

In the heart of a quaint town named Willowbrook, there stood an old-fashioned bookstore called 'Read & Reconnect'. As the mighty Amazon emerged, foot traffic dwindled and the store's future began to look uncertain. But the bookstore's owner, Norma, was determined not to let her beloved establishment fade into oblivion. She realized that Read & Reconnect had something that Amazon couldn't replicate—a sense of community, personal touch and the joy of browsing physical shelves.

Norma embarked on a mission to fight back against the Amazon tide. The first step was to reimagine the store's layout. Norma transformed sections of the store into cosy reading nooks, complete with comfortable seating, warm lighting and inviting decor. These nooks became spaces where customers could not only discover new books but also immerse themselves in their reading journeys.

Next, Norma introduced regular book clubs and reading circles. People of all ages started coming together to discuss their favourite reads, share recommendations and build friendships around a shared love for literature. The bookstore buzzed with conversations, laughter and a renewed sense of community. Norma's team partnered with local authors to host book signings and writing workshops. The store became a hub for creative expression, attracting aspiring writers and fostering a sense of collaboration between authors and readers.

The centrepiece of the local literary renaissance, however, was an annual event called 'Willowbrook Literary Festival'. The festival brought together authors, artists and book enthusiasts from near and far. The town square turned into a bustling fairground of bookstalls, creative workshops and literary performances. The festival celebrated the magic of storytelling and strengthened the bonds within the community.

Winning Propositions for the Physical Store

In the excitement of e-commerce, with online retailing grabbing an increasing share of the retail dollar, it is easy to write an obituary of the traditional brick-and-mortar stores. There is no denying that we will see fewer 'traditional' stores since their value proposition for shoppers is becoming less compelling relative to online platforms. This is especially true for the developed world, which has, for example, too many department stores and will continue to see store closures. Similarly, more bookstores, travel agents and bank branches will disappear if they have not already done so. Yet, it is also undeniable that there is, and will continue to be, a role for physical stores. It is just that traditional brick-and-mortar retailers need to dig deep into consumer insights to understand when they have a reason to exist and how they can meet shopper needs that online retailing cannot fulfil.

This chapter examines when and what type of physical stores add value over e-commerce for shoppers. Specifically, convenience stores, airport duty-free outlets, low-price stores such as club stores, hard discounters or outlet malls will continue to thrive. High street shopping will be challenged, with its high-cost structure, but can succeed in a relatively few global tourist destinations. For other traditional brick-and-mortar chains to survive the customer migration to online sales, their physical stores must be reinvented to become more experiential as well as more integrated with an omnichannel proposition.

Convenience Stores: The 'Nearest'

A recent survey found that Americans are in love with convenience stores (c-stores). Over seven in ten adults aged eighteen and over claim to discover new products and brands in c-stores.[1] Nearly four in ten shop at c-stores at least twice a week, and nearly two-thirds visit at least once a week.[2] This may seem surprising in an e-commerce world. However, when you are making coffee at home and run out of milk, or need an immediate drink to hydrate yourself, the nearest c-store is the solution. Their easily accessible 'round the corner' location, quick in and out process and speedy transactions comprise a powerful value proposition.

When surveyed, 65 per cent of American consumers considered 'location' as the prime reason for their preference for c-stores.[3] In addition, 43 per cent said that they lived within a mile of a c-store; in rural areas, more than eight in ten residents (86 per cent) said that these locations were within ten minutes of their home and were often the only places in town to buy grocery items, fuel, other products and services.[4] These stores often become the focal point for communities and provide essential services for nearby residents, including food, fuel, financial and postal services and click-and-collect of online orders from Amazon.

Even in the e-commerce dominant world, c-stores continue to deliver unique benefits to their customers. Shoppers perceive c-stores as meeting their immediate needs (59 per cent); conducting transactions quickly so customers can be on their way fast (54 per cent); providing good value for their budget despite being more expensive than supermarkets (30 per cent); offering a good variety of products within the limited space (28 per cent); and being less crowded and thus easier to navigate (34 per cent).[5]

What do shoppers purchase at c-stores? Two-thirds (67 per cent) of Americans buy candy; 57 per cent purchase on-the-go drinks like coffee, tea or fountain beverages; 40 per cent buy milk, juice and other staples; 32 per cent buy packaged beverages; and 23 per cent buy beer. In addition, while in the store, 30 per cent tend to buy prepared foods and 37 per cent purchase lottery tickets.[6]

C-store chains such as 7-Eleven have prospered despite their relatively premium price strategy, with 12,000 locations in North America alone and 78,000 locations worldwide. Moreover, the chain is operating in only nineteen countries. The global potential for 7-Eleven seems relatively untapped, although global c-store chains struggle in emerging countries because of the ubiquity of mom-and-pop operated stores in these markets. The entrepreneurial local corner stores in less developed parts of Africa and Asia usually pay no rent (spread out on sidewalks or inherited leases at minimal rents), few wages (employ family members, who get no official monthly salary) and sometimes, not even electricity charges (as a wire is illegally pulled from the streetlights). Although, with economic development, this situation will change, the proposition for the 'nearest' store continues to remain strong in an e-commerce world. All that c-stores need to do is continue executing on the basic proposition. Globally, c-stores are estimated to have revenues of $2 trillion and an annual growth of more than 5 per cent.[7] There is always the need for the 'nearest' in retail.

Airport Duty-free Stores: The Captive Audience

Airport duty-free stores offer captive consumers—travellers with few other alternatives for retail or entertainment—a way to kill time and indulge themselves. The growth in airport stores was driven by the increasing numbers of airline passengers as low-cost carriers brought air travel within the reach of the masses. Prior to the pandemic, which decimated air travel, the global airline industry had almost five billion scheduled passengers.[8] With increasing congestion and security procedures, the longer waiting times at airports make travellers more open to greater engagement with retail and brands. In contrast, in most developed countries, footfall numbers on the high street are declining.

Initially, duty-free shopping was conceptualized as offering a limited number of highly taxed products at lower prices than the high street. Airports now have a much wider offering, from traditional luxury brands to mass-market products offered by a WH Smith or Boots. Duty-free airport spaces have become increasingly sophisticated and now include restaurants, bars, hotels and even beauty centres and massage parlours. Consequently, it mirrors the high street shopping centre or a small mall.

While consumers still perceive 'tax-free' to imply cheaper prices, this is not necessarily true. Duty-free operators are under no obligation or regulation to pass on the tax savings to shoppers. As a result, different airports and operators demonstrate dramatically different prices for an identical product. A quick check by the author for a Toblerone bar of 360 gm at various airports found it priced at $8.13 at London

Heathrow, $12.87 at Bangkok, $15.50 at Newark, $16.00 at Nairobi, $17.27 at Singapore and $20.43 at Mumbai (converted to US$ based on the exchange rate of the day).[9] Oh, by the way, you can purchase it at a Tesco physical store in London for £5 or $6.25! This is for a product that is manufactured in a single location, so there are no differences in quality and the shipping costs are negligible.

In 2022, global duty-free retail sales were estimated at $70 billion, with an annual growth rate of 10 per cent.[10] It is the second fastest-growing retail channel after online. Clearly, as demonstrated by the Toblerone analysis above, prices are not the driver of this growth. There are many consumer motivations beyond perceived lower prices, which have led to the popularity of airport duty-free shopping. For travellers, who are usually stressed before an upcoming journey, it is easier and quicker to buy a product they need at the airport than on the high street. Similarly, gift shopping for family and friends is easier to do at the airport than spending precious holiday time. Furthermore, as consumers are investing more in travel and leisure experiences, they are more inclined to spend during holiday or business travel. On these occasions, the shopper's mind is not so much on economizing, but rather on giving themselves a treat. In addition, sometimes there are items, like limited-edition products, that are specifically designed for and only available in duty-free airport stores.

Of course, the popularity of online shopping and smartphones has had an impact on duty-free shopping. Consequently, the duty-free industry is evolving, with many operators having introduced the ability to place online orders that can then be picked up in-store at the airport. In Asia, given the dominance of Chinese tourists, Alipay payments have been enabled at checkout counters, and mobile loyalty points are automatically added to Singapore's iChangi or Heathrow Rewards apps.

Easy access to a premium audience which is usually time-starved, but at airports with a 'dwell time' between check-in and boarding, has attracted the attention of upscale brands.[11] For example, The House of Suntory is promoting its brands and whiskies through an immersive gallery at Changi airport, while Prada launched its new fragrance at Heathrow with an interactive screen. Helsinki Airport organized a runway fashion show with seven top European and Asian designers. The Italian sunglass maker Luxottica reported that its 155 airport stores are the best performers out of all its 3000 retail locations.[12] As they say, 'captive' customers are the best shoppers.

First Price Stores: The 'Cheapest'

Are prices cheaper offline or online? Many consumers believe that prices are cheaper online, and respondents on websites like Quora explain this by noting the lack of real estate costs and cheaper operations for online retailers.[13] Several academic and popular studies have examined this. It turns out that the answer is more nuanced. When the cost and hassle of shipping an online order for a retailer is greater than the benefits that an online retailer enjoys (e.g., lower real estate costs), prices will be lower at physical stores.

A large-scale study comparing offline and online prices of fifty-six multichannel retailers in ten countries across 24,000 products found 72 per cent of the prices to be identical.[14] The differences depended upon the type of product and the retailer's positioning strategy. Here, we assume delivery fees as additional charges, thereby increasing the prices for online purchases while ignoring any costs of visiting the physical store. This is consistent with how most customers perceive this.

For customers who do not consider the time and effort required to visit a physical store a cost, the best prices may be available offline for low-value items, given the cost of picking and delivering online orders, except for digital products. As previously discussed in Chapter 5, groceries and drugstore items are the best examples of this. A shopper in India who compared prices of a month's worth of groceries at DMart (physical store) with the online retailers Amazon, Flipkart, BigBasket and Grofers, observed that the DMart bill of Rs 2378 was lower than that of the online retailers, where it varied from Rs 2804 at Grofers to Rs 2990 at Amazon.[15] This was a substantial difference and it was calculated before considering any delivery charges levied by the online retailers.

In summary, in the product categories where the cost of offering delivery and returns is high on online orders, some retailers choose to ignore the e-commerce route and focus on giving the best price to their in-store shoppers. For price-sensitive customers, this is incentive enough to favour the physical stores over the convenience of online buying. On the other hand, in product categories such as computers or sporting goods like golf clubs, where the picking and delivery costs are relatively small (in absolute dollars) compared to the gross margin dollars generated on their sale, the online prices are lower.[16] Here, the online retailer benefits from the lack of premises, with its associated rental and operating costs. However, even for such products, there is a segment of shoppers who are willing to pay more for the service and advice they receive in offline stores.

Retailers like Aldi, Costco, Lidl and Trader Joe's, whose value proposition is to offer the best prices to their shoppers, tend to not pursue online sales aggressively. They instead offer customers, who come to their physical stores, the excitement of a treasure hunt—by offering unique products or/and great cost savings. For example, according to a retail analyst, roughly 20 per cent of Lidl's centre aisle is devoted to 'Lidl Surprises', an array of unexpected non-food items such as diaper bags and dress shoes. He said, 'These items are available in limited quantities and rotated weekly with the aim of driving a treasure hunt mentality. Once they're gone, they're gone.'[17] For now, online shopping will not put a dampener on such price-driven retail outlets that provide shoppers with compelling reasons to visit their physical stores. Both Aldi and Lidl are booming, with more than 11,000 and 12,000 stores globally and sales at $100 billion annually.[18]

Unlike Walmart's aggressive push into e-commerce, most deep discounters eschewed online sales. Aldi and Lidl did not have any online sales capability. Given their success and fast growth, they did not see the need to engage with online shoppers for profit-dilutive sales. Similarly, Dollar General, USA's largest discounter, with 19,000 locations and revenues of $37.8 billion, as well as Dollar Tree, with annual revenues of $28.75 billion, were unenthusiastic about e-commerce.

The pandemic, however, changed all this. Now all of them have e-commerce, encouraging click-and-collect or home delivery through partners like DoorDash and Deliveroo. But their focus remains on walk-in customers to the store as their price-sensitive shoppers are unlikely to pay extra for home delivery. At Costco, while overall sales for the first three quarters of the financial year 2023 increased by 5.5 per cent over the previous year to $160 billion, e-commerce sales over the same period declined by 7.8 per cent.[19] As a share of Costco's total revenues, online sales have declined since 2020 as their customers have returned to the stores for the physical experience.

Similarly, discount stores such as T.J. Maxx, Burlington and Ross acquire premium apparel brands' excess inventory cheaply and then offer them to customers at bargain prices. TJX is a company that has mastered the treasure hunt experience. It continues to grow by sticking to its strategy of offering new and limited assortments at unbeatable prices. Since loyal shoppers are aware that TJX's offerings may not be around tomorrow, they frequently visit the store to see what is available and buy right then. As Tara Miller, Trader Joe's vice president of marketing, observed, 'While other retailers were cutting staff and adding things like self-checkout, kerbside pickup, and outsourcing delivery options, we were hiring more crew and we continue to do that . . . [to help customers] find our next great product just as they've always been.'[20]

Outlet stores are another example of a physical retail format that creates value for their customers through store visits. Outlets have come a long way since their origin in the 1930s when their primary purpose was to sell 'slightly' damaged or excess goods at a cheap price. Now, they have expanded into outlet malls, which have become destinations for shoppers. At these outlet malls, top brands offer last season's or specially formulated merchandise at discounted prices. As a result, shoppers find great deals not only by mainstream fashion apparel brands like Gap or Hanes but also by luxury designers like Burberry, Gucci and Prada. The wide range of shoppers that such brands target has led to over 400 outlet malls across the US alone.[21]

Outlet 'bus trips' have gained popularity as a form of tourism. Bicester Village, an hour out of London, has become one of the biggest tourist attractions in the UK, with 160 designer brand outlets (started with thirteen in 1995). Since 2015, it has even had its own train station to facilitate the travel of 7 million visitors annually, a third of whom are international tourists. A visitor, on average, ends up spending over four hours in the village, which has numerous cafes and restaurants, including a club where non-shopping spouses can chill.[22] Shoppers benefit from discounts offered, but visitors also see it as a fun outing. Retailers use predictive pricing models by combining rich customer data with advanced analytics to ensure that what they offer in terms of prices and promotions is consistent with what their shoppers seek. For many shoppers, being the 'cheapest' is incentive enough to visit the store.

High Street of Major Tourist Destinations: The Time-Rich Shopper

Shopping tourism is when travellers visit a destination for the primary purpose of purchasing goods or when shopping is a large part of the planned holiday activities at the destination. China, ignoring the pandemic hiatus, is the world's largest outbound tourism market, with 155 million-plus outbound trips and $255 billion (a quarter of the global tourism spend) of travel spending in 2019.[23] Chinese tourists, like other emerging market travellers, are new to overseas travel and, thus, prefer to check off major Western cities in North America and Europe, like London, Paris, New York and Milan, on their bucket list, instead of visiting more esoteric adventure destinations.

It has been found that 90 per cent of Asia's population and 85 per cent of the population of Western Europe prefer shopping tourism.[24] Shopping at physical stores is a major motivation for travel and online sales are not an option in these circumstances. In-store shopping is viewed as a fun and social activity while on holiday. Moreover, tourists from emerging markets often find the prices and selection in major Western cities to be better than in their home country, especially for upscale brands, where taxes tend to be high on imported products.

Asian tourists account for a large proportion of the sales of luxury brands in major Western cities. Over 50 per cent of sales of high-value goods in Europe are to foreign tourists.[25] As a result, many brands are employing people with Chinese and Russian language skills at their stores in London, New York,

Paris and Zurich. Yet, even as the impact of the pandemic dissipates, the high street continues to struggle. It will undergo a transformation in terms of the types of retail outlets in the developed markets. High-traffic tourist shopping centres will hold their proposition with respect to physical stores for luxury brands. Some of the buzz has returned to Fifth Avenue in New York, Bond Street in London, Orchard Road in Singapore, Bahnhofstrasse in Zurich and Ginza in Tokyo. However, online sales have impacted the traditional retailers, like department stores, that used to vie for space on these streets. This has resulted in the softening of rentals, and empty storefronts that are now visible on even London's famed shopping mecca, Oxford Street.

Between outlet malls and the high street is the destination mall. American Dream, East Rutherford, New Jersey is advertised as, 'There's really nothing like it. It's a real destination shopping experience where you'd go to spend the day.'[26] The country's largest mall, covering more than 3 million square feet, includes a theme park, an NHL-sized ice rink, a water park and North America's first indoor ski and snowboard park. Its experiential stores, with special offerings and designs, include lululemon and Hermès flagship stores.[27]

Many other examples exist in America, a country with the space to execute this format, such as the Mall of America in Minnesota, which attracts more than 40 million visitors a year. It includes an aquarium, an indoor Nickelodeon amusement park and two attached hotels, besides more than 500 stores.[28] Forum Shops at Caesars in Las Vegas, a larger-than-life concept with light shows and moving statues, comprises art galleries, restaurants and high-end retailers. Ala Moana Center in Honolulu, Hawaii, the world's largest open-air shopping centre, is especially popular with Asian visitors, who make it their first stop in the US.[29] Call it 'shoppertainment'.

Can Department Stores Survive?

There was a time when department stores were fashionable places for cool people to hang out at. I fondly remember shopping at what was then Marshall Fields on Chicago's magnificent mile. With their proposition both aspirational, like Bloomingdale's or Macy's, and having mass appeal, like Sears and JCPenney, the department stores targeted a substantial segment of the population. However, the last two decades have not been kind to them. Department stores have been under attack from retail formats that offer four enduring values—the cheapest, the biggest, the nearest and the best.

- The discount format, with its cheap and cheerful formula, has been led by Walmart in the US. But, more recently, the hard discounters, led by Aldi, Dollar General, Family Dollar and Dollar Tree, have also been gaining ground.
- Category killers such as IKEA, PetSmart and Best Buy have the biggest assortment of products for the person looking to shop within a category, especially in specialist categories viewed as destination shopping.
- Traditionally, the nearest space was occupied by the c-stores and mom-and-pop stores. Now, Amazon is the nearest, and if convenience is what a shopper is looking for, then it is hard to beat.
- The 'best' is the only proposition that department stores are left with, and in fact, this has always been core to them. However, leading designers, like Calvin Klein or Hugo Boss, are increasingly opening their own branded stores in major cities, while speciality retailers like Sephora and Zara are also competing as 'best' in the traditional high-margin categories for department stores.

Not surprisingly, the department store chains are suffering from considerable turmoil as they seek a sustainable model in the new retail world. The solutions pursued to avoid going bust or merging are predictable. Assortment optimization—deciding which categories and merchandise to flog to protect margins in the face of high location and staff costs—is clearly the initial response. For example, electronics and toys have either disappeared or their space has been dramatically reduced in department stores. These product lines cannot be sustained in the face of competition from discounters, online retailers and category killers.

The need to focus on high-margin and unique merchandise has led to an explosion of private labels. While private labels do deliver margins, they rarely have the same upmarket snob appeal that comes with selling exclusive designer or luxury merchandise. Often, department stores have to complement private labels with designer merchandise that has high margins, both in absolute and percentage terms.

If you can't beat them, joining them is another approach taken by many US department stores as they open up outlet stores such as Bloomingdale's Outlet or Nordstrom Rack. This strategy helps them sell Overruns, unsold end-of-the-season merchandise and some dedicated lower-priced lines in less expensive locations with minimum staff intensity. While this strategy can deliver additional profits, to a large extent, its success is based on how successful the full-price chain stores are. That is the umbrella under which outlet stores have the cachet of being a bargain hunter's dream. If the store cannot sell at full price, the low-price value proposition holds less appeal to the customers.

Many traditional department stores are aggressively pushing online sales, and some have been more successful than others. For example, it is reported that John Lewis in the UK gets

33 per cent of its sales online, compared to only 15 per cent of Marks & Spencer. It is doubtful that these online sales can be as profitable as the store sales unless customers are willing to pay the full shipping costs. For John Lewis, given that they sell many white goods, this may be true as customers are used to paying for shipping even when buying in-store and thus, they can be more readily persuaded to defray the full cost of delivery for the retailer. However, only some of these online sales are truly additional sales; the rest cannibalize the store sales, lowering sales per square foot and the viability of the physical stores.

In the final analysis, department stores have realized that the market for their format has shrunk considerably in the face of new alternatives for the shopper. A study reported that in 2015, sales per square foot for department stores in the US was $1.65, 24 per cent less than in 2006![30] The fact is that we need a lot fewer department stores, at least in developed countries. Another US-based study indicated that 800 stores, or one-fifth of the anchor space occupied by department stores, need to be shut down for the sales productivity to be acceptable.

The most profitable and sustainable proposition for department stores is to be premium/high-end retailers, such as Nordstrom in New York or Selfridges in London, located in cities that are popular tourist destinations. Here, they serve as entertainment experiences, and include food and wellness options. But how many such stores do we need? Many department store chains have no choice but to close their underperforming stores and in quite dramatic numbers.

Shutting down stores is never an easy decision. The leases are usually long-term and a store could be yielding positive cash flow. If the lease has to be bought out, it means instead of keeping a store that is cash-positive, the retailer has to make a cash-negative decision. Furthermore, the corporate overhead would now be spread over fewer stores. Therefore, the easier decision is to leave them open despite the stores being unprofitable. However, because these stores will ultimately be shuttered, investment is no longer poured into them. This only makes them shabby, with a detrimental impact on the shopper experience, sales and image. The challenge to find a relevant and differentiated proposition for department stores continues. There are many opinions, but the data is clear—we need a lot fewer of them in the developed world.

The decline of department stores has impacted malls in the US. Consider that in the 1980s, 2500 malls, anchored by department stores, accounted for more than 50 per cent of US retail. But between 2016 and 2020, mall cornerstones like JCPenney, Macy's and Sears closed 1050 stores.[31] Today, only around 700 malls survive in the US.[32] The growth of e-commerce and the rise of Generation Z, which grew up wedded to a digital world, have led many to argue that malls in the US will continue to see further closures. Yet, there is hope for the remaining malls provided they can pivot to delivering the experience demanded in the face of online shopping instead of seeing it as a battle for supremacy.

The previous department store and apparel focus of malls must yield to offering more entertainment opportunities like movie theatres, beauty spas, fitness centres and luxury retailers as well as destinations for food and drink. Malls must reinforce the social aspect, the third place, where one can hang out with friends, avoiding the rain, heat and cold, compared to walking in the park or being shushed in the library. The evidence suggests that the digital Generation Z understands the unique value that malls deliver. For example, in July 2023, 78 per cent of Gen Z (born mid to late 1990s) visited a mall compared to 70 per cent of millennials (born early 1980s) and 48 per cent of Gen X (born mid to late 1960s ending early 1980s) respondents.[33] Mall traffic was up 12 per cent in 2022 over 2019 for malls located in upscale areas and 9 per cent for lower-tier malls.[34] Clearly, physical stores can fight back and find success. Even direct-to-consumer online companies like Allbirds, Warby Parker and Wayfair are opening retail stores, realizing it helps expand the target market and acquire new customers. Regardless, fewer but better is the prognosis for malls and department stores.

Reimagining the Store for Deep Experience

The brick-and-mortar store has been under threat from online shopping for two decades now. We now have enough experience to know that physical stores do add value if positioned correctly and imagined differently. E-commerce has an important limitation as it falls short of physically engaging customers. This is the playing field on which physical stores can win. As James Daunt, the CEO of Barnes & Noble, queried, 'How is it that bookstores do justify themselves in the age of Amazon?'[35] He answered, 'They do so by being in places in which you discover books with an enjoyment, with a pleasure, with a serendipity that is simply impossible to replicate online.' After a decade of contraction, Barnes & Noble is planning to open new stores.

A survey of 50,000 customers finds that 'the critical role of the physical store is to enhance customer value by providing physical engagement customers need to purchase 'deep' products'.[36] Deep products come bundled with services and experiences and require ample inspection for customers to make an informed decision. The brick-and-mortar stores provide the right interface ('physical engagement') for customers to buy deep products.[37] Table 7.1 lists the many ways in which the physical store can motivate the shopper to visit the store.

Stores (unless they fall into one of the previously discussed categories such as c-stores, airport duty-free, first price) have to

Table 7.1. Reasons for Visiting Physical Store

Reason	Customer Seeking...	Examples
Discovery	Expensive products	Cars, luxury brands
	Unfamiliar	New products, fashion items
	Unstandardized	Fruits and vegetables
Convenience	Location access	Convenience stores, airport duty-free
	Search ease	Proximity to other stores to aid comparison
	Quick possession	No waiting time
	Transaction flexibility	Pay cash, layaway
Customization	Retailer-driven	Adjust skis before delivery
	Customer-driven	M&M to create unique mix, alterations
	Co-creation	Spectacles, hearing aids, fitted kitchen
Community	Active	Shop with family and friends
	Passive	Apple classes, coffee shops with sofas
Shoppertainment	Product-related	Book signings, fashion shows
	Product-unrelated	Santa at store, store decorations

Source: Adapted from Els Breugelmanns et al., 'The Future of Physical Stores: Creating Reasons for Customers to Visit,' *Journal of Retailing*, in press.

move beyond simply selling products to justify their existence. They must become more than simply a point of transaction. They must become places where consumers get *relevant, differentiated* and *credible* experiences that are impossible to deliver satisfactorily online. Relevant means they should be a great fit with the target market of the brand store or retailer. Differentiated requires they should offer experiences that are better or different from those available at competitors and online. And, finally, credible implies that the brand is seen as being authentically linked to the experience offered. With large assortments, attentive and informed services and additional value-adding activities that are integral to the brand proposition, many retailers are successfully pursuing this strategy. They have created a reason for consumers to visit the store regardless of the online retail.

Examples include:
- CAMP, a family experience store in the US. It is a toy store with an innovative concept—the excitement of shopping for a toy outweighs buying it online. Camp stores have theme-based interactive experiences like Travel Camp, Cooking Camp and Toy Lab Camp, where children can play accompanied by adults. While it is free to play in Camp's stores, the walls, tables and even the floors are packed with toys available for purchase.
- In 2019, lululemon opened a new flagship store in Lincoln Park, Chicago. 20,000-square-foot store spread over two floors, the store has a yoga studio, gym, meditation area and cafe. Customers can also take strength training or high-intensity workout classes in the store.[38]
- Sephora offers classes in skincare, brow shaping, contouring and make-up. Specific classes target customers who identify as non-binary and transgender as part of their 'Classes for Confidence' initiative.[39]
- Canada Goose enables customers to experience what it is like to wear their products in the environments they were created for. In some of its stores, it has installed Cold Rooms, which are set to -25 degrees Celsius (-13 degrees Fahrenheit), and are also equipped with a wind chill button.[40]
- Nike's flagship store in New York City is six storeys tall, with each floor offering customers different ways to interact

with the brand. For example, one floor stocks products based on hyper-local customer preferences, another contains a Sneaker Lab, where customers can witness new sneakers being made, while another allows customers to customize their own sneakers.[41]

- House of Vans is a store with a concrete skating bowl, a ramp and a street course for customers to use, as well as a music venue, a cafe and bar, an artist incubator space and a movie theatre.[42]

These retailers have carefully designed their experiential activities to reinforce the distinctiveness of their brand and bring to life their unique selling proposition for the shopper. The result is that despite the 8 per cent decrease in foot traffic at sporting goods apparel stores, lululemon and Nike stores continue to see 11 per cent and 6 per cent higher traffic, respectively.[43] Many other retailers have adopted this strategy of encouraging repeat visits by offering customers more than just products. For example, every six to eight weeks, STORY reinvents its entire space, from store design to inventory, around particular themes.[44]

Of course, it would be remiss not to mention the most successful of all retail stores when evaluated on sales per square foot basis—the Apple store. The key aspect of Apple stores is their focus on community engagement. A programme called 'Today at Apple' hosts in-person classes and workshops for people wanting to learn creative activities like photography, videography, music, art and design. 'Teacher Tuesdays' at Apple stores is an initiative designed to help educate working teachers on how they can better incorporate technology into their classrooms.[45] Apple's new generation stores, launched in 2022, even include boardrooms that visiting entrepreneurs may use to meet and discuss their ideas, and they hold coding workshops—called 'Hour of Code'—for kids, teaching them Apple's programming language, Swift.[46]

The variety of services Apple offers in its stores, such as the Genius Bar—where a dedicated team assists customers in fixing and troubleshooting Apple products—and other in-store events, combined with staffing its stores with knowledgeable and helpful experts and its sales consultants' ability to roam the store freely to help customers, makes the Apple store a destination. Apple provides all its store associates with extensive training that leads to well-rounded product knowledge, enabling informed interactions with shoppers.[47] In contrast, at many stores, one gets the feeling the shopper knows the product better than the sales associate. While the Apple store makes for a great example to be used by professors and consultants, its generalizability is limited. Apple store strategy and execution are enabled via high margins, unique brand positioning and resale price maintenance. In contrast, most retail is a cut-throat, low-margin business that sells commodity products. As such, many retailers cannot afford to create the service differentiation and store atmospherics of an Apple store. The customers are simply unwilling to pay for it. The larger point of this discussion is that, while acknowledging that sales will continue to migrate online, there remains a role for the physical store if they reinforce at least some of the attributes listed in Table 7.1. It is not that the physical store is dead, it just needs to evolve for the omnichannel shopper.

The Omnichannel Shopper

The point we keep driving is that the future is omnichannel. Going forward, all consumers will shop at both offline and online stores. As mentioned earlier, in the US, 92 per cent of all Amazon customers also made a trip to Walmart in the same year, while many Walmart shoppers are migrating to online channels to fulfil some of their needs. In 2022, as previously mentioned, Walmart itself generated $82 billion of online sales globally, or 13.5 per cent of its overall revenues, up from 5 per cent only five years ago.[48] This omnichannel shopping behaviour allows the physical store chain to coexist in an increasingly online-centric retail world.

A study of 46,000 consumers found that around 73 per cent of respondents prefer to shop through multiple channels.[49] Comparatively, only 7 per cent of consumers shop online exclusively and 20 per cent shop merely in-store. While the 20 per cent that shop exclusively in-store is expected to decline, there will remain a segment that prefers to shop in-store. In response, Jumbo, a Dutch supermarket, introduced 'Chatter Checkout'—slow checkouts for people who enjoy chatting. It helps the elderly who, in many ageing countries, must deal with loneliness.[50] It proved so successful that Jumbo rolled it out to 200 stores.

Retail therapy is a well-documented phenomenon, usually associating shopping with improving the buyer's mood. Physical stores can play a crucial role in addressing one of the larger problems afflicting society, that of loneliness. Most Americans report experiencing loneliness. The United States Surgeon General, Dr Vivek Murthy, argued that loneliness is as harmful as smoking fifteen cigarettes a day and worse than consuming six alcoholic drinks daily.[51] To address the issue, Japan and the UK have appointed ministers for loneliness to address this issue. As people get older (more likely survive their partners), wealthier (less need to cohabit) and consume more social media (encourages unhealthy comparison of one's life with the curated life of others), they feel social isolation.

Physical retailers should embrace this problem as an opportunity and introduce talking cafes, community volunteering events and chatty benches. Parks in Australia,

Britain and Sweden have adopted chatty benches, with signs encouraging strangers to sit there and talk to each other. Recall that malls and stores shelter people from crime and the elements that a park bench may not; it is a natural advantage for brick-and-mortar stores. That the physical store is losing relevance in the digital marketplace may be the conventional wisdom, but it is better seen as a call for reinvention in the omnichannel world.

The overall retail trend in terms of a greater proportion of sales going online is clear. Yet, it is omnichannel, with webrooming and showrooming, which is becoming ubiquitous. Webrooming refers to the phenomenon of many customers, especially for products like automobiles and real estate, browsing online for research. However, when it comes to making an actual purchase, they prefer to do it in person at the physical outlet. Customers like establishing a relationship with the automobile dealer, as they need future servicing. A real estate broker helps organize the viewing and complete the transaction. A survey by Google reinforces this by finding:[52]

- 88 per cent of shoppers research online before making a purchase.
- The ubiquity of smartphones means customers research online while physically doing in-store shopping.
- Online behaviour influences 56 per cent of all sales made in-store.
- Desire to physically touch and try the product is the most cited reason for preferring physical stores.

Showrooming is the opposite—shoppers check out the merchandise in physical stores, but then place their orders online. Surveys found that 56 per cent of shoppers visit physical stores to first see, touch and feel products before they buy.[53] Information search is followed by price discovery. This is frequently the case for products such as clothes, electronics, furniture and white goods. Even though online fashion retail is booming, physical stores in high-traffic areas succeed because consumers want to see, feel and assess the fit of their clothes before they buy them. However, for staples (e.g., innerwear, T-shirts), which are repeat buys, online is increasingly preferred.

Changing customer expectations and technological advancements are allowing retailers to become more sophisticated in serving omnichannel shoppers. Consider Home Depot, the most successful home improvement store chain in the US, with $157 billion in revenues in 2022. They have two types of customers—tradespeople and do-it-yourself (DIY) consumers—each of whom contributes half of the total revenues for the retailer.

Tradespeople frequently purchase large quantities of merchandise, rarely require advice and know the store intimately. When shopping online, they do not have the time to sit with laptops or tablets, instead preferring the mobile phone. What they need to know is product specifications, price and whether there is availability in contractor-like (large) quantities at the store, often for click-and-collect on their way to the job site.

The DIY consumer, unless they are buying bulbs or paper towels, is usually engaged in a once- or twice-in-a-lifetime project like remodelling the kitchen.[54] These are 'e-commerce unfriendly' products. They need to come into the store for advice and to help figure out, for example, whether they prefer a granite or a quartz countertop. To serve this need, the consumer heads to the nearest brick-and-mortar store, seeks advice and then, if they so desire, the Home Depot staff member, who is equipped with a smartphone, will place an order on behalf of the consumer for home delivery. Alternatively, some customers want to think about it and need to measure the space at home accurately. These customers can complete the transaction online when they return home.

The rise of online retailing, combined with the relentless assault from Amazon and Walmart, has had a deleterious impact on physical store chain economics. The loss of customer traffic, the higher costs of fulfilling online orders and the increased costs (e.g., rentals, staff) of operating physical stores have decimated sales per square foot to unsustainable levels. The clash between Amazon and Walmart has demonstrated the saying 'when elephants fight, the ants perish'. To thrive in the face of this clash between, and against, these giants, physical stores must have a compelling proposition to attract store visits.

As the examples in this chapter demonstrate, there are retail store concepts that are less impacted by online retail, such as convenience stores, airport duty-free, hard discounters, club stores, outlet stores, destination malls and even some highly tourist-frequented high streets. They thrive because of their distinctive value proposition, which complements the shopper needs served by online retail. Other store formats, such as department stores, malls and speciality stores, must reinvent themselves to deliver deep in-store customer experiences, such as Apple, lululemon and Sephora do to entice shoppers. Otherwise, their future is bleak—between 2016 to 2019, Amazon converted twenty-five disused malls into fulfilment centres!

Chapter Takeaways

- Despite being seen as being in an existential crisis, physical stores do have a future beyond simply supporting the omnichannel operations.
- Many brick-and-mortar formats such as bank branches, travel agents as well as book and music stores do not have

any distinctive value via-a-vis online retail. They have mostly closed and will continue to decline.

- Formats such as convenience stores, which offer a complementary proposition to online, airport duty-free shops that serve captive customers, or hard discounters, club stores and outlet malls that incentivize consumer store visits through lower prices, continue to thrive in the digital age despite limited e-commerce offerings.

- Speciality high street stores, department stores and malls are being challenged to offer a deep experience that only a physical store can uniquely deliver vis-a-vis online. If they are unable to do so, there will be continued restructuring of these chains, with store closures.

- The Apple store, on a sales per square foot basis, is the most successful physical retail store format. However, it is unlikely that other retailers can use them as an inspiration. Apple uniquely commands brand equity, differentiated products and high margins on premium-priced products as well as the ability to practice resale price maintenance. Retail, in contrast, is overwhelmingly a low-margin business selling commodity products with lots of competition.

- Physical store chains must learn to serve omnichannel customers who increasingly indulge in webrooming (research online, buy in-store) and showrooming (research in-store, buy online).

8

The Clash for the Future in India

In the vibrant land of Bharatville, two retail giants, Amazon and Walmart, embarked on a journey of competition to reshape the Indian retail landscape.

Amazon, the digital marvel, had already established itself as a familiar name in the country. Its online marketplace had captivated Indian consumers with its vast selection, convenient delivery options and a personalized shopping experience. Shoppers could explore a plethora of products, from electronics to fashion, all from the comfort of their homes.

On the other side of the spectrum was Walmart, known for vast hypermarkets that offered a wide range of products under one roof. Its Indian venture, FlipMart, aimed to combine the physical shopping experience with the convenience of e-commerce, enticing customers with the promise of a seamless omnichannel experience.

The competition extended beyond the virtual and physical realms. Amazon and Walmart each invested in India's fast-growing digital payments landscape, with Amazon Pay and PhonePe, respectively. This not only facilitated transactions but also solidified their positions as integral players in the country's evolving financial ecosystem.

Amid the rivalry, both Amazon and Walmart recognized the importance of localization. They adapted to the cultural nuances of Bharatville, offering customer service in regional languages, catering to diverse preferences and celebrating India's festivals with tailored offerings.

The culmination of this competition was a win for the people of Bharatville. The presence of Amazon and Walmart drove innovation, improved customer experience and expanded opportunities for both consumers and local businesses.

Emerging Markets are Different

It is important to make the distinction between developed and emerging markets. Emerging markets, despite seeing growth in online sales, are also experiencing a spurt in modern physical stores as they are relatively under-stored markets. In Asian countries, alongside the increasing popularity of e-commerce, unorganized traditional retail stores and wet markets are currently transforming into modern retail chains.

The declining retail footfall and large-scale closures of physical storefronts in the developed world should not lead to a generalization of this phenomenon across the world. In emerging markets, there is considerable hunger among the population for the modern physical retail format. In countries such as India, Indonesia, Myanmar and even China (though less so), the retail landscape is still evolving from the unorganized sector to more modern formats. This is happening in parallel with the growth of e-commerce, and consequently, the competition between online and offline is not seen in zero-sum terms in these markets.

As an exercise, Table 8.1 examines the store penetration of three popular global chains, IKEA, Starbucks and Inditex (primarily Zara), across the ten most populous countries (ignoring Russia). These also happen to be retail chains that are less impacted by e-commerce. Taking the US as the benchmark for a developed retail market, it is obvious that there is considerable room for growth for these three retailers in the other markets. In the US, there is an IKEA store for every 6 million people, a Starbucks store for every 20,000 and an Inditex store for every 3.3 million. After the US, the greatest penetration by these chains is in China, where there is an IKEA store for every 39 million, a Starbucks store for every 2,30,000 and an Inditex store for every 4.6 million (see Table 8.1). In other words, to equalize the stores per million, IKEA, Starbucks and Zara would have to increase their stores in China by around 6.5 times, 11 times and 1.5 times, respectively!

As the per capita income in China continues to increase, this market will be ready for IKEA and Starbucks to at least double the number of their stores in the country over the next decade. Despite being arguably as sophisticated an e-commerce market as the US, retail store chains, both international and domestic, see tremendous opportunities to expand their physical footprint in China. No wonder then that in 2020, IKEA planned to make its biggest annual investment in China, more than $1.4 billion, to expand its physical presence.[1]

Relative to China, the lower per capita income in India makes the country less attractive for global retailers. However, after two years of the pandemic, local retail chains have made a spectacular comeback in 2022. One of India's largest retailers, DMart, has added fifty new stores, with plans to add another 135 stores in the 2023–24 fiscal year.[2] Other Indian retail chains like Aditya Birla Group, Titan and Tanishq, V-Mart and Westside have aggressive store openings planned. Avenue Supermarts, the fourth-largest chain of convenience stores in India, is also looking to scale up from 284 to 1500 stores.[3]

Table 8.1. The Store Penetration of Three Popular Global Chains

Country	Population millions	IKEA		Starbucks		Inditex	
		Number of stores	Millions population per store	Number of stores	Millions population per store	Number of stores	Millions population per store
India	1,400	5	280.00	270	5.19	24	58.33
China	1,400	36	38.89	6,000	0.23	303	4.62
USA	329	55	5.98	15,952	0.02	99	3.32
Indonesia	271	7	38.71	480	0.56	63	4.30
Pakistan	217	0	NA	0	NA	0	NA
Brazil	211	0	NA	122	1.73	39	5.41
Nigeria	200	0	NA	0	NA	0	NA
Bangladesh	163	0	NA	0	NA	0	NA
Mexico	128	2	64.00	531	0.24	440	0.29
Japan	126	12	10.50	1,415	0.09	86	1.47

Reliance Retail, the largest retail player with its twenty-two sub-brands in a variety of formats, including consumer electronics, grocery as well as fashion and lifestyle, saw a 30 per cent growth in both retail revenues ($21 billion equivalent) and profits for the 2023 fiscal year.[4] The Reliance strategy is to enter a new sector in a big way with lots of capital and then tweak the business model or format to get it right. In contrast, the retail operations at the Tata group, led by Noel Tata, start a new format with a few initial stores and perfect the model before scaling up. This approach is best seen with the Zudio stores, launched in 2016.[5]

Most retailers have concentrated on the Tier 1 and Tier 2 cities in India, ignoring the rest as not having adequate purchasing power. In contrast, Zudio deliberately focuses its attention on towns such as Imphal, Gorakhpur, Pathankot and Ujjain, which lack modern sophisticated retail. Yes, it reminds one of Walmart's initial years in the US. Concentrating on selling fast-moving clothing items that are affordable yet aspirational for its core target of younger couples, the chain now has approximately 500 stores across the country and is reportedly generating revenues of $300 million. Realizing that the cost of delivery and returns would be formidable and unsustainable for such a model, the chain ignores e-commerce. Like Aldi, it avoids malls and instead selects standalone, cheaper locations with lower costs. Despite economizing on fit-out costs for these locations, it offers a premium retail experience.

As the most populated country in the world with an average age of twenty-eight years (relative to forty-eight in Japan, thirty-seven in China and thirty-eight in the US), India is primed to increase shopping in physical stores. The growing young population means India leads the world in the number of hours spent per week (10.42) reading books. As a result, unlike the developed markets, where bookstores have disappeared for the most part, one can still see bookstores in India. Yes, online sales are exploding in India, but this does not mean that physical store chains are declining, as our examples of DMart, Reliance and Zudio demonstrate.

The story of India—low per capita income, large young population, lower Internet penetration and smaller presence of modern physical store chains—is also true for other emerging markets like Indonesia, Vietnam and Bangladesh. The growth of physical stores is also driven by the service preferences of consumers in Asian markets. In Indonesia, Eyvette Tung, JD.ID's head of offline business, said, 'It's a service culture. Indonesian shoppers are not independent and prefer not to be. You see in other places like China that everyone is going online so quickly, but people in Indonesia want that interaction, and they like to be served. That is a big reason we're ramping up efforts offline, even as we build out our online infrastructure.'[6]

In Egypt, while consulting for Commercial International Bank (CIB), a leading bank, I was surprised to learn that their bank branches were flourishing. In London, on the street where I live, there used to be four bank branches, but now there are none. It turns out that many Egyptians prefer to go to the branch for transactions. CIB, which charges a small fee for in-person branch transactions, claims that its branches are profitable. Similarly, in Malaysia, a survey by KPMG found that three out of four Malaysian shoppers believe that online shopping is for convenience, while shopping at physical stores is for pleasure.[7]

Africa, even further behind with respect to modern trade, is expected to explode as a growth opportunity for physical store retailers over the next twenty-five years. In 2050, ten of the most populated cities in the world will be in Africa, up from five currently.[8] In summary, the relative importance of physical retail to e-commerce will continue a downward path in the developed markets as a percentage of total retail sales. One thus expects to see more physical retail store restructurings as well as a decline in their revenues in absolute dollar terms. In contrast, while the share of online retail will increase in emerging markets, it may not come at the cost of reducing the absolute dollar sales from physical retailing. The growth in consumption will lead retailers to continue to add new physical stores for the foreseeable future in emerging markets. As retailers seek growth globally, the only two economies large enough to rival the US in sales one day are China and India.

The Futility of China

Despite the success of IKEA, Starbucks and Zara in China, both Amazon and Walmart have struggled in the country. An important reason is that both these retailers' consumer proposition is based on the lowest prices, which is hard for them to reproduce in China. Western brands are perceived as high quality, which contradicts the value proposition of the two retailers. But, more importantly, they must compete against well-funded local competitors who understand the domestic market better and know how to operate in China at low costs. As a result, a foreign retailer will be unable to replicate its home country cost advantage in China against the local competitors.

Enamoured by the size of the China market, Walmart began operations in 1996 with a store in Shenzhen. It operates both Supercenter and Sam's Club formats. Despite pouring money and making strategic acquisitions, the number of Supercenters has fallen from 424 in 2018 to 361 in 2022. They have had more success with Sam's Club, which has grown to thirty-six stores from nineteen over the same period. For e-commerce, Walmart has partnered with JD.com since 2016 and this has allowed them to provide one-hour delivery service.

Overall, after twenty-seven years, Walmart in China, with $13.85 billion in revenues for 2022, is struggling to make a significant impact or at least meet the expectations that the company had for the country when it entered. However, to Walmart's credit, it has hung in there and is present in around 100 cities. In contrast, the French global hypermarket chain, Carrefour, has essentially withdrawn from the country. The Walmart Supercenters are challenged to become profitable as well as meet Chinese shopper expectations, but Sam's Club is demonstrating smart growth.

Amazon entered China in 2004 by acquiring Joyo.com, a leading book and media online retailer at that time. It was renamed Amazon China and Bezos was excited about the opportunity. Amazon steadily expanded its range of products and delivery options. However, the challenge for Amazon was not dissimilar to that faced by Walmart. As retailers (unlike brands such as IKEA, Starbucks or Zara), they essentially sell the same products that are available at local retailers. Given the local knowledge that Alibaba, JD.com, Taobao and Tmall have, combined with the laser focus on China as their domestic market, Amazon could not effectively compete. The Chinese rivals often offered free shipping without requiring shoppers to meet a minimum order size, as well as many promotions. Furthermore, both Amazon and Walmart have had to face capricious investigations regarding poor quality and counterfeit products in their assortments. Finally, with only a 6 per cent share of Chinese online retail in 2019, Amazon decided to withdraw from the Chinese domestic e-commerce business.

The list of foreign Internet competitors who have failed in China, even those who have pioneered and lead their respective concepts globally, is too long for it to be a random occurrence. Think Amazon and eBay versus Alibaba; Facebook versus WeChat; Google versus Baidu; and Uber versus Didi.

I recall having dinner at an upscale Michelin-star restaurant in Shanghai with a set of the most powerful local Chinese investors a few years before Uber pulled out. One of them dismissively observed that Uber had no chance of succeeding in China. The smart money knows that the government has a hand in tilting the playing field against overseas Internet firms in favour of local entrepreneurs. The flip side of this is that the protected domestic market has not prepared the Chinese Internet giants for competing in overseas markets.

India: A Must-Win Market

Since China is off the table for e-commerce, India, given its large population and growth prospects, has been designated as a 'must-win' market by both Amazon and Walmart. It is the next battleground after the US. For both companies, India represents the most attractive potential market globally—perhaps the only market available to the two retailers that could one day rival the US in size in terms of revenues. While Walmart has struggled with physical stores in both China and India compared to what they believed initially was the promise, the e-commerce industry in India, which is expected to reach $350 billion by 2030,[9] has become the retailer's focus.

Online shopping in India, on an accelerated upswing since 2017, was further boosted by the pandemic. The country has the third-largest online shopper base globally, with 180–190 million shoppers in 2021, including 50 million new shoppers (added in the year). The online cohort is growing rapidly; analysts estimate that India may overtake the US in the next couple of years and by 2027, reach an online shopper base of 400–450 million. While historically, the focus has been on categories such as mobile phones, electronics and appliances, in recent years, Indian shoppers have taken to buying other categories online as well, such as fashion, general merchandise categories (including personal care) and groceries.

Apart from the pandemic, this surge in e-retail in the country can be attributed to three key factors. The first is improvements in technology that provide faster Internet speeds and higher security when sharing financial details online. The second reason is greater access to the Internet through smartphones, even in Tier 2 and Tier 3 cities. Three of five online shoppers today belong to Tier 2 or smaller cities, while one in five belongs to low-to-middle income segments.[10] And finally, growth has been spurred by practices such as aggressive marketing by the e-commerce players through advertising, discounts and offers such as cash-back guarantees. This has been further enhanced by offering cash on delivery options as credit cards are still relatively rare and consumers are wary that the product will be actually delivered. Of course, online retailers also offer the usual fast delivery, easy access to global brands and low prices.

Walmart had entered India in 2007 through a joint venture with Bharti Enterprises, an Indian business conglomerate, and opened wholesale stores. After the joint venture dissolved in 2013 due to allegations of having broken US anti-bribery laws, Walmart set up its wholly owned subsidiary, taking full control of its stores. Its stores, called 'Best Price', are membership-based and cater to a B2B market, targeting *kiranas* (neighbourhood grocery stores), other small and medium businesses as well as institutional buyers such as hotels, restaurants and offices.

In 2023, Walmart was India's largest cash-and-carry business, with twenty-eight Best Price stores across nine states in the country supporting more than 1.5 million members.[11] Yet, the slow scale-up is demonstrated by the fact that in the past three years, Walmart was stagnant at twenty-eight physical stores and is present in only nine out of twenty-eight states. The cash-and-carry business in India is restricted to selling to small businesses. Consumers do not have the same access to cars and out-of-town locations as in the US. In addition, this wholesale business competes against traditional Indian wholesalers who work on minuscule (2–3 per cent) margins. The large FMCG companies, having observed how retailers turned the tables on them in the developed countries, are resistant to providing higher margins to large formats like Walmart—even if serving Walmart has a lower cost-to-serve for suppliers and the retailer has higher buying power or scale. Thus, there is no real opening for a Walmart to cut prices against the established traditional wholesale and retail players.

The battle between Amazon and Walmart in India is more in the e-commerce arena. Amazon entered the Indian market in 2013. Under the country's FDI policy at the time, foreign e-commerce players could not sell directly to consumers online. Hence, it initially set up operations as Amazon Seller Services, a marketplace for third-party sellers of Indian-made products. Over the years, Amazon has adapted its product-to-delivery ecosystem considerably to cater to the Indian business environment. For example, in 2015, it launched Amazon Chai Cart to educate small business owners about the benefits of e-commerce and onboarded over 10,000 sellers across thirty-one cities.[12] It also introduced Amazon Tatkal, offering traditional sellers a suite of online launch services such as registration, imaging, cataloguing and sales training. It enables small and medium businesses to get online and sell on Amazon.in in less than sixty minutes.

Another of Amazon's India-centric services is Easy Ship, whereby Amazon picks up packaged goods from a seller and delivers them to consumers, and Seller Flex, in which sellers assign a part of their own warehouse for products sold on Amazon while the e-retailer undertakes the delivery process. For delivery, besides tying up with local courier services in the country, the company set up its own subsidiary, Amazon Transportation Services, in 2016. In 2017, it introduced its food retailing operations after getting the green light from the government of India.[13] The company enlists the numerous mom-and-pop stores in Tier 2 and Tier 3 cities that define the retail sector in India as its delivery partners, especially in rural and remote areas of the country. It plans to scale its presence to 160 cities, up from 100 cities in 2019.[14]

A recent Amazon initiative is the launch of 'Smart Stores'. More than 10,000 shops, ranging from mom-and-pop stores to big retail chains, including Big Bazaar, MedPlus and More Supermarkets, have deployed the company's software to maintain a digital log of the inventory they have in the shop along with a QR code. Consumers can scan this QR code with the Amazon app to see all the products and any discounts that the shop offers, check customer reviews and even select and pay using Amazon Pay.[15] These 'digital storefronts' offering omnichannel services are a win-win for both consumers and shop owners.

Amazon India's e-commerce platform has over 1 million sellers offering 168 million products, with over 4000 products being sold on it per minute. The retailer has over 5 million Prime subscribers.[16] In 2022, Amazon operations in India comprised Amazon Marketplace, Amazon Internet (AWS), Amazon Wholesale, Amazon Data, Amazon Pay and Amazon Retail. Together, they account for an operating revenue of $5.56 billion. Its Marketplace contributes $2.8 billion in revenues and makes a loss of $834 million, while the retail segment accounts for $224 million in revenue and $105 million in losses[17] (refer to Table 8.2).[18]

Observing Amazon's e-commerce entry into the country, in 2018, Walmart made a major commitment to India. It acquired 77 per cent of Flipkart, India's leading online retail company,

Table 8.2. Amazon India Performance

In billion rupees	Revenue			Profit/Loss		
Company	FY22	FY21	Change	FY22	FY21	Change
Amazon Pay	20.00	17.20	17%	-17.41	-15.16	-15%
Amazon Marketplace	214.62	162.00	32%	-36.49	-47.48	+23%
Amazon Retail	17.10	15.85	8%	-7.94	-6.50	-22%
Amazon Wholesale	45.92	36.18	27%	-4.80	-.1.62	-196%
Amazon Data	35.40	25.51	39%	3.27	1.31	+150%
Amazon Internet	89.56	54.05	66%	-0.02	0.18	-113%

In billions of rupees
Source: https://entrackr.com/2022/09/amazon-indian-ecosystem-in-fy22-5-56-bn-income-and-834-mn-loss/.

for $16 billion plus an additional $2 billion committed for growth investments. At that time, Flipkart had more than 100 million registered shoppers, more than 50 million on its mobile app, and owned several e-commerce companies, notably Myntra (fashion e-retailer), Letsbuy (electronics e-retailer), eBay India and PhonePe, a mobile payments app based on the Indian government-backed Unified Payments Interface (UPI).[19] For the then latest year ending 31 March 2018, Flipkart had net sales of $4.6 billion and a GMV of $7.5 billion.

At more than four times sales, revenue observers perceived that Walmart had paid way too much for Flipkart, essentially a retailer making losses. However, the entire acquisition needs to be seen from the perspective of the clash between Amazon and Walmart. In 2018, the Walmart market cap was languishing at around $200 billion, unchanged from 2010, despite annual revenues running at $500 billion. In contrast, Amazon had a market cap of $800 billion and heading to a trillion dollars, despite sales of only $180 billion. The problem was Walmart's lack of a growth story.

The cumulative annual growth rate (CAGR) for Walmart during the five-year period from 2012 to 2017 was 1.3 per cent, down from the 4.1 per cent CAGR for 2007–12. Essentially, Walmart's revenues had plateaued, while Amazon's CAGR for the same years was 23.8 per cent, down from 32.7 per cent. Walmart investors were spooked and repeatedly questioned the Walmart management on the growth prospects, arguing that in the absence of a growth story, the Walmart stock price was doomed.

Walmart's international operations outside North America, notably Europe, had not proved successful. There was enough evidence that the hope of China and India being growth platforms equal to the US via physical stores was also not going to happen. The acquisition of Jet to drive Walmart's e-commerce transformation in the US had been an integration challenge as the Jet team had refused to move to Bentonville from New York. As a result, there were few options for Walmart.

Scanning the globe, it was clear that with the core business growth stunted at 1 per cent, the only realistic option available was to buy into India through Flipkart. Post-acquisition, Walmart had a growth narrative to share with the markets: we have the leading online retailer in the third-largest market in the world which is exploding in terms of online users. Adding Flipkart sales to Walmart's online revenues also made the global e-commerce number for Walmart look more respectable. Post-acquisition, the market cap of Walmart leapt to $300 billion by the end of 2018. It has also helped the subsequent five-year (2017–22) CAGR to recover to 4.5 per cent.

In 2022, Walmart's operations in India comprised Flipkart Internet (business-to-consumer platforms including Myntra,

PhonePe, etc.) and Flipkart India (business-to-business platforms, including its Best Price stores). Its online retail caters to more than 350 million users and has more than 3,00,000 sellers offering 150 million products across eighty product categories. Its wholesale business supports 1.6 million kiranas, selling them bulk purchases across categories, including grocery, general merchandise and fashion. PhonePe has become India's largest online payments platform, with more than 300 million users and more than a billion transactions per month.[20] In 2022, the Flipkart Group's revenue was about $8.13 billion, with Flipkart India at $6.73 billion and Flipkart Internet at $1.4 billion.[21]

Currently, Walmart plans to focus on growing its e-commerce presence in India through its existing businesses and not open any more physical stores in the country.[22] To further increase its share in Flipkart (from 77 per cent), Walmart acquired the remaining shares worth around $1.4 billion in 2023 from minority investors.[23] India is the only market where Amazon is number two in terms of its e-commerce. It is estimated that Walmart-owned Flipkart leads, although marginally, and the two retailers together control about 60–70 per cent of India's e-commerce market. In FY 2022, during the festival season, Flipkart reported a GMV of $23 billion to Amazon's $18–20 billion.[24]

Over the last decade, Amazon has invested over $6.5 billion in the country's e-commerce, and despite losses, it plans to spend nearly $13 billion more by 2030, its largest-ever investment since it began operations in India.[25] While India is the large must-win market for both these giants, from a financial perspective, it has been a brutal battlefield. Despite billions of dollars invested over a decade into acquisitions and growth, both firms continue to make considerable losses with no profits in sight. This reinforces the strategic nature of the Indian market for Amazon and Walmart. These two firms are large enough that the financial costs, albeit in billions, have only a minimal impact on the overall fortunes of the firms. Think of it like R&D investments by manufacturers. Even if most new products fail, leading firms devote 3–5 per cent of their annual revenues to R&D in the hope of securing the future.

The clash between Amazon and Walmart will be simultaneously played out in India and the US. However, unlike in the US, where Walmart has a large physical presence, in India, it is pursuing an e-commerce first strategy. And unlike the US, where Amazon leads Walmart in online sales, in India, Amazon lags behind Flipkart in the e-commerce business. However, my own analysis is that Amazon is building a stronger fundamental business relative to Flipkart.

Flipkart, in its attempt to pump up the GMV number, has concentrated on mobile handset sales. Despite the large ticket size, these handset sales are unprofitable. In contrast to 25–30 per cent of Flipkart revenues coming from handsets, Amazon has closer to 10 per cent. Emphasizing fashion, Amazon India has chosen a laser focus on the customer experience. Relative to Flipkart, Amazon delivery is faster, more accurate and executed with greater certainty. The customer service is superior and the returns are processed more easily. The competition in India will continue to be a direct clash between these two giants because of the online focus of both retailers. But one must not forget that India has other players competing in retailing, most notably Reliance. Unless Flipkart improves its strategy and execution, my prediction is that it will rapidly cede the online retail space to Amazon, and the clash in India may become more Amazon versus Reliance.

Chapter Takeaways

• Many emerging markets are at an earlier stage of retail development and will see parallel growth both in e-commerce and physical stores. Even formats that are declining in developed markets, like bank branches, supermarkets and department stores are growing in markets such as India and Indonesia.

- China has been a tough market for both retailers as domestic competitors have an advantage against international competitors who sell similar products and brands. There also seems to be an unwritten policy to favour local e-commerce and gig economy players.

- India has become a must-win market for both Amazon and Walmart. Despite sustained large investments in India over a decade as well as occupying the number one and two positions for e-commerce, both firms have only losses to show for their efforts so far.

- Leading manufacturing firms, despite the high failure rates for new products, invest 3–5 per cent of their annual revenues in R&D to secure the future. Amazon and Walmart's investments in China and India are market development costs in the hope of securing their future growth.

- The slight lead Flipkart has over Amazon in revenues must be balanced against the superior long-term orientation and execution of Amazon. It is more likely a clash between Amazon and Reliance in India if Walmart does not improve operations.

9

Incumbents versus Disruptors

In the ancient realm of Eldoria, where kingdoms and cultures thrived, a tale of rivalry unfolded that would forever shape the destiny of the land. The tale pitted the established incumbents, representing the old ways, against the disruptive newcomers, the 'Barbarians at the Gate'.

At the heart of Eldoria stood the mighty city of Prospera, a bastion of tradition and wealth. The city was home to legacy industries that had long held sway over the land's economy. The Guild of Artisans, the Merchant Consortium and the Kingdom's Mint were pillars of Prospera's prosperity, ensuring the continuation of age-old practices and sustaining the status quo.

But change was brewing on the outskirts of the land. Tribes of nomadic tribespeople, known as the Barbarians at the Gate, had begun to harness new techniques and technologies that challenged the very foundations of Eldoria's established order. These barbarians had learnt to harness the power of fire and metal, crafting tools and weapons that were more efficient and effective than the guild's traditional methods.

As the smoke of innovation rose from the barbarians' forges, word reached Prospera of their advancements. The guilds dismissed these newcomers as mere upstarts, scoffing at their new-fangled ideas and branding them as threats to the city's way of life. The established leaders, ensconced in their comfort, believed that the barbarians would remain confined to their distant territories.

However, the barbarians were driven by a thirst for change and an appetite for progress. Fuelled by their new technologies, they began to trade with neighbouring villages, expanding their influence and disrupting the long-standing supply chains. The villages, recognizing the benefits of these innovations, welcomed the barbarians and their newfound tools.

As the barbarians' sphere of influence grew, they found themselves at the very gates of Prospera. The city's leadership, now alarmed by the speed of change and the extent of disruption, convened a council to assess the situation. They realized that the barbarians were not just a minor inconvenience; they were a transformative force that threatened to reshape Eldoria's landscape.

The council faced a dilemma: to resist or to embrace the changes brought by the barbarians. Some advocated for fortifying the city's walls, clinging to tradition in the hope that the barbarians' momentum would wane. Others, recognizing the inevitability of change, proposed a more daring approach— to welcome the barbarians, learn from their innovations and forge a new path for Eldoria's future.

Ultimately, the city's leadership chose the path of adaptation. Prospera opened its gates to the barbarians, inviting them to showcase their technologies and share their insights. The guilds and consortium, once resistant to change, began to collaborate with the newcomers, merging old wisdom with new knowledge.

Over time, the distinction between incumbents and disruptors began to blur. Eldoria became a land where tradition and innovation coexisted harmoniously. The city of Prospera, once insular and resistant to change, became a beacon of progress that drew traders, artisans and innovators from neighbouring realms.

Amazon versus Walmart

The battle between Amazon and Walmart is reflective of the more general competition between traditional incumbents and emergent disruptors. Think automobile rental companies versus Uber, sprawling hotel chains like Marriott versus Airbnb, Hollywood studios and distribution companies versus Netflix as well as television networks such as ABC and NBC versus Google and Meta. The established firms see these upstarts as barbarians at the gate, initially puzzled by their strategy, competitive advantage, business model and financial viability.

The traditional firm views itself as a long-standing pillar of the industry because of its strong brand equity based on the existing customer franchise and profitability, while having rewarded shareholders with consistent dividends. Yet, the disruptors often command much larger market capitalization despite sometimes limited or no profitability. This is frustrating for the incumbent firms. As they see it, they have assets, brands, customers, distribution networks and profits, but apparently no love from the financial markets. Moreover, these innovative disruptors seem to elude the glare of anti-trust authorities and regulators despite having what appear to be winner-take-all strategies and monopolistic positions.

To conclude this book, let us investigate more deeply, abstracting from Amazon versus Walmart, the differences between incumbents and disruptors on strategy (exploitation versus exploration), business models (products versus platforms) and financial mindset (profit versus shareholder wealth maximization). Finally, let us end with some observations on the prospects for these two influential companies, Amazon and Walmart, who have redefined consumer behaviour and the retail industry, and, as a consequence, business and brands.

Exploitation versus Exploration

From a strategy perspective, the fundamental difference between Walmart and Amazon is in their core competence (the distinctive capability of a firm)—exploitation versus exploration. Incumbent firms like Walmart have perfected exploiting an existing business model. They have faced relatively low uncertainty with respect to the markets, technology, systems, products and customers. They have well-developed models focused on efficiency and growth across this familiar competitive landscape. Repeated decisions born out of their planning and experience, and executed with discipline, have resulted in a steady stream of profits for the firm and dividends for the shareholders.

The culture at incumbent firms is biased towards predictability and seeks to minimize failures. Using the established hierarchy, they repeat decisions that have worked well in the past. This implies that any innovation, change and risk-taking is constrained, in terms of ideation as well as implementation, within efficient planned processes. These firms are geared for incremental innovation, finding small hits to improve their business model and execution. The managers who run these organizations are experienced in the industry and have strong planning, execution and control skills, ensuring that expected performance is delivered on time and on budget.

Disruptors like Amazon have mastered exploration and the ability to search for new, breakthrough business models. They have operated under high uncertainty with respect to what is the industry definition, how to create stickiness with customers and finding a viable business model. Their model is closer to venture capital, exploring numerous vectors through small and large investments. The novel decision-making process is biased to be rapid, iterative and experimental. It is supported by a culture that has a high tolerance for failures. However, out of these experiments and failures comes learning and adaptation. These disruptive firms frequently 'pivot'—change strategic direction and/or business model.

The disruptors are geared for radical innovation—big bets in the hope of gaining dominant positions in newly defined and unfamiliar competitive spaces that potentially result in great rewards. The managers who run these organizations are explorers and love the excitement and challenge that come with the unknown. They can live with ambiguity, turn on a dime when needed, abandon existing positions and refocus constantly between the big picture and the details needed for execution. This is not only how the successful Amazon Prime, AWS, Amazon Marketplace and advertising were born, but also how several physical store formats of Amazon were launched and then abandoned. Table 9.1 demonstrates that Amazon's list of failures is long, including Amazon Auctions, Fire Phone, Myhabit.com, Amazon Spark and Amazon Tap.[1] According to Bezos, 'I believe we are the best place in the world to fail, and failure and invention are inseparable twins. To invent you have to experiment, and if you know in advance that it's going to work, it's not an experiment.'[2]

It is important to remember that companies like Walmart that are viewed as incumbents today were once considered innovators. As noted earlier, Walmart in the 1970s and 1980s had changed the face of retail in the US. Both companies have been highly innovative on all the fronts that define a successful business: product, process, management and business model. As Figure 9.1 demonstrates with examples rather than an

Table 9.1. Sixty Failures of Amazon

Name	Description	Started In	Closed In
Fire Phone	Smartphone	2014	2015
Dash Buttons	For the ease of repeat ordering of certain products	2015	2019
Pets.com	Pet supply website	1998	2000
Amazon Auction	Its version of eBay	1999	2001
Amazon Destinations	Local getaway travel agency	2015	2015
Myhabit.com	Membership-only e-store with flash sales	2011	2016
LivBid.com	Online auction platform	1996	2001
BuyVIP	Member-only luxury goods e-commerce	2006	2010
BookSurge	Publishing platform with on-demand book printing service	2000	2005
Whole Foods 365	Supermarket chain	2016	2019
Amazon Unbox	Movie downloading platform	2006	2015
Kozmo.com	Online retailer providing quick and efficient delivery of goods	1998	2000
TextPayMe	Peer to peer payment portal	2005	2006
Amazon Storywriter	Online screenwriting platform	2015	2019
Amazon Payphrase	Online payment system	2009	2012
Amazon Local	Marketplace for local deals	2011	2015
Amazon Tap	Early version of Amazon Echo	2016	2018
Endless.com	E-commerce for shoes and accessories	2007	2012
Shelfari	Social cataloguing website for books	2006	2016
Amazon Spark	Social commerce platform	2007	2019

Name	Description	Started In	Closed In
Amazon Restaurants	Food delivery service	2015	2018
Yap	Speech recognition system	2006	2011
Withoutabox	Website for filmmakers to distribute films	2000	2019
Wing.ae	Delivery service	2016	2017
Amazon Webstores	For merchants to build their websites	2010	2015
Amazon Webpay	Online payment system	2011	2014
Amazon Wallet	E-wallet	2014	2015
Touchco	Touch screen technology	2009	2010
Amazon Tickets	Ticketing platform for public events	2015	2018
Amazon Test Drive	App for users to try apps without downloading	2011	2015
TenMarks Education	Personalized online math programs	2009	2019
TeachStreet	Marketplace for local/online classes	2008	2012
SnapTell	Visual product search technology	2006	2009
Shoefitr	Online shoe-fitting software	2010	2016
Safaba	Automated translation software	2009	2015
Rooftop Media	Comedy live performances platform	2006	2014
Reflexive Entertainment	Online game distribution service	1997	2010
Quidsi	E-commerce with super-fast delivery and elevated customer service	2010	2017
Amazon Pop-up Stores	Physical spaces that sold Amazon's products	2014	2019
PlanetAll	Social networking site	1996	2000
Partpic	Visual technology to identify industrial parts	2013	2016

Name	Description	Started In	Closed In
OurHouse.com	Online home goods retailer	1999	2001
Mobipocket	Reader software for eBooks	2000	2017
MindCorps Incorporated	Software and consulting company	1996	1998
LoveFilm	DVD rental and video streaming provider	2002	2017
Amazon Local Register	Wireless card reader	2014	2016
Liquavista	Solutions for less battery power	2006	2018
Junglee	Price comparison shopping service	1996	2017
Amazon Instant Pickup	Enabled orders collection at pre-selected locations	2017	2018
Amazon Fresh's Local Market Seller	Initiative to sell grocery products from third-party vendors	2007	2018
Egghead Software	Computer store selling products at low prices	1984	2001
Amazon Cloud Player	Cloud storage for music	2012	2015
Bookpages	Online bookstore	1996	1998
Avalon Books	Book publisher for romance and mystery novels	1950	2012
Amazon AskVille	Online Q&A platform	2006	2013
Amie Street	Online indie music store	2006	2010
Amiato	Data analysis and business intelligence tool	2011	2014
Alexa.com	Web traffic analytics service for users who installed Alexa's toolbar	1996	2022
Crucible	Multiplayer third-person shooter game	2020	2020
Haven	Healthcare cooperative venture	2018	2021

Source: https://www.failory.com/blog/amazon-failures.

exhaustive view, Amazon and Walmart have both been responsible for bringing new substantial innovation to markets and business practices.

Figure 9.1. Innovation at Amazon and Walmart

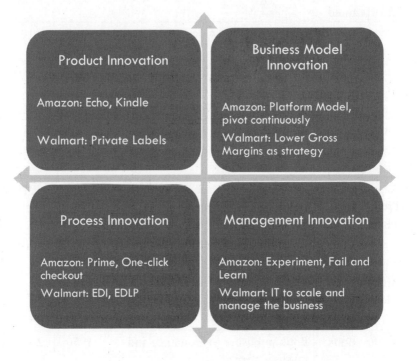

Once the new business model is established, the firm then settles into incremental innovation. The history of innovation in organizations and industries is defined by spurts of radical innovation with long periods of incremental innovation between them. And the wheel of retailing we referred to earlier in the book suggests that Amazon will one day become the incumbent and a new radical form will be, or perhaps already is, born to challenge it. No firm is a greater contender to these two giants than TikTok (owned by China's ByteDance) and its sister

Chinese company Douyin. Douyin has already grabbed 10 per cent of retail e-commerce sales in China, with sales revenues expected to top $300 billion in 2023. While TikTok Shop has made great strides in South-east Asia, especially Indonesia, with sales to its young users via live-streaming and brand storefronts. In the US, despite concerns by the government, TikTok has managed to surpass 150 million users. They have finally launched TikTok Shop in the US with optimistic projections as globally, the average TikTok user spends ninety-five minutes a day on the app!

Products versus Platforms

At the level of the business model, or how a firm makes money, Amazon and Walmart could not be more different in their initial launch. Amazon thinks and is conceptualized as a platform business. On the other hand, Walmart's domination is a result of its relentless execution of the product business logic.

As we learnt in the chapter on Walmart, its business model adds the least possible gross margin (to cover Walmart's operating costs and profits) to the cost of goods sold (which is paid to its suppliers). With its large scale, it is to be expected that Walmart receives the best prices from suppliers. As a result, Walmart offers the most competitive prices (the sum of the costs of goods sold plus gross margin) to their customers. By keeping its operating expenses under tight control and benefiting from positive scale economies, Walmart keeps growing; the retailer makes small margins in percentage terms, but steadily increasing profits in absolute dollar terms.

In contrast, Amazon is built as a platform that connects vendors with online shoppers in an open architecture. None of the profits, as we learnt in the previous chapters, are generated through buying and selling—the online retail business that observers tend to see as defining Amazon. Instead, it is the audience of marketplace vendors and shoppers on the Amazon platform which is monetized via commissions on marketplace sales and advertising.

Furthermore, to run its online retail business, Amazon needed to invest in cloud and delivery infrastructure. Unlike a product logic company, which would have seen these assets as proprietary capabilities to be shielded from the world, Amazon converted them into additional platforms that are monetized through AWS and offer fulfilment by Amazon (FBA) as a service to other vendors, regardless of whether they are on Amazon Marketplace or not. Unlike Walmart, Amazon, because of its platform thinking, views its investment in the delivery infrastructure as more than simply building a competitive moat. The cloud and delivery infrastructures are set up not only to generate revenues but also to bring additional scale to these activities, which, in turn, lowers the cloud and delivery costs for Amazon's retail business too.

Fundamentally, the incumbents and disruptors are different. Incumbents follow a perfected, established product business model, while disruptors pursue the logic of building successful platforms. Table 9.2 delineates the differences between product and platform models on several dimensions and starkly demonstrates why traditional product firms are puzzled by the disruptor platform models.

The product model is based on concepts that are traditionally taught as underlying best business practices—a laser focus on customer needs, seeking competitive differentiation, knowing that the only source of cash is ultimately the customer, and carefully monitoring the profitability of customers and products. In contrast, platform models pay equal attention to the players on multiple sides of the transaction (e.g., buyers and sellers at Amazon, drivers and riders at Uber, restaurants,

Table 9.2. Product versus Platform Models

	Product	Platform
Design	Customer needs	Customers + suppliers needs equally
Competitive	Product features: differentiation	Network effects: 'winner take all'?
Revenue	Primarily single: exchange products for cash + some services	Usually multiple: access charge + advt + ranking + support
Monetization	Customers	Customers (Netflix); suppliers (eBay); audience (Facebook); all (Amazon)
Profit	On firm and individual transaction; profit maximization model	On suppliers and number of transactions; wealth creation model
Cost	Primarily variable cost, margins	Primarily fixed cost, scalability
System	Closed loop—'control'	Open loop (plug and play)—'empower'
Marketing	Traditional push + pull	Primarily word of mouth pull
Customer switching	Minor	Major
Manager	Cost + quality	Connection + gravity + flow
Examples	Apple pre-2003; Walmart	Apple post-2003; Amazon

delivery workers and customers at Just Eat) to meet their objective of dominating transaction volume and achieving default industry status.

The size of the network drives platform revenues, resulting in the firm occupying a dominant position, which is then rewarded by high market capitalization. These disruptive firms believe that if adequate audiences are attracted to the platform, monetization eventually follows. Thus, they and their investors are willing to tolerate, as in the case of Amazon, long periods of loss-making operations. These losses are seen as the cost of building the network. Profits, once they appear, grow exponentially because platforms are a fixed-cost business. On achieving scale, additional customers can be served at almost zero marginal costs. In contrast, product businesses like Walmart are variable-cost businesses. For every additional sale, 75 per cent of the marginal revenues must be paid out to the suppliers by Walmart. Scale has relatively limited effects on this linear financial model.

Managers who run incumbent firms prefer control over their operations and build 'closed loop' systems. They attract customers by using traditional marketing tactics of push (promotions) and pull (advertising). Knowing that customers can switch easily to competitors (e.g., from a Walmart store to a Target or Costco), these firms closely monitor their own costs and quality to ensure that they keep delivering higher value to shoppers.

Disruptors are predisposed to 'open loop' systems, as Amazon does with AWS and FBA. They empower those on their platform by providing them with tools to create value because of the size of their network. For example, Amazon enables the sharing of customers' reviews and Google provides easy-to-use tools to evaluate advertising returns. Disruptors, especially successful ones like Amazon, Google and Meta, prefer not to spend on traditional marketing, relying primarily on word of mouth. Once on the platform, customers are unlikely to switch. For example, one could move to another platform from Facebook, but then one would have to convince all their friends, and their friends and so on, to move too. Similarly at Amazon, a Prime subscription, a one-click checkout facility and personalized recommendation increases customer switching costs.

Unlike the product firm's focus on cost and quality, managers of platforms worry about 'connection'—how easy it is to sign up to the platform, 'gravity'—how successful it is in drawing a large audience and 'flow'—how painless and secure it is to transact with others on the platform. Given the winner-take-all character of platforms, they are in a race to build their networks. Concerns about profitability are muted at the scale-up stage of these firms.

Profit Maximization versus Shareholder Wealth Maximization

Incumbents and disruptors differ in how they keep score and assess whether they are performing better or worse than in previous periods or against competitors. Because of the differences in strategy and business model of these two types of firms, their financial model and mindset also differ.

The profit maximization approach of incumbents, born out of neoclassical economics, emphasizes the efficient use of resources, which is reflected in the difference between a firm's revenues and costs. Firms in this world view exist to maximize profits and use this criterion to evaluate their managerial decisions (e.g., build a new factory, or enter a new business or market). The non-efficient firms fail when they are unable to generate profits and are competed out of the market. The profit maximization criterion provides managers clarity on the goal (maximize profits) and the process (invest in efficient activities).

The profit maximization model followed by firms like Walmart has the advantage that managers are incentivized based on what they control. However, the profit criterion brings clarity only on the short-term objectives; what creates profits in the long run is more ambiguous. The danger is that firms focus more on initiatives, projects and businesses that yield short-term profits at the cost of long-term investments to future-proof the business. Furthermore, as we have often seen, profit is a judgement, capable of manipulation by managers in concert with auditors. In general, it is hard to account for intangibles (e.g., brand, dominant positions or reputation) in profit-maximizing models without making at least some arbitrary judgements of value. Similarly, the risks or volatility associated with a pattern of returns is usually ignored.

In traditional firms, the assumption is that profit maximization over time leads to wealth maximization for the shareholders. This view was best summarized by Milton Friedman as 'there is only one and one social responsibility of business—to use its resources and engage in activities designed to increase profits so long as it stays within the rules of the game'.[3] The adoption of the profit maximization approach served firms well until the changed focus on shareholder value creation espoused by Alfred Rappaport and Michel Jensen in the late 1980s.[4] The shareholder value creation approach underlies platform models.

The shareholder wealth maximization approach of disruptors focuses on growth and gaining a dominant industry position. Firms in this world view exist to maximize returns to shareholders and consider the market as the most efficient mechanism for allocating capital, with the stock price the best estimate of future cash flows. Firms fail when they are unable to attract equity investment. This approach has clarity with respect to the goal of maximizing shareholder value, but considerable ambiguity on how to achieve it.

The shareholder wealth maximization model pays more attention to cash flow than profits. Amazon is the poster child of this approach—the retailer has made huge losses over its lifetime, especially during the first decade of operations. Yet, the market has rewarded it for taking moonshots. In theory, incentives between owners and managers are aligned (focused on stock returns), reducing the agency problems rife in profit-maximizing organizations. Furthermore, unlike profitability, it is more difficult for managers to manipulate the stock price. It also encourages long-term orientation, with clear benchmarks (stock market performance of comparable companies) available to assess performance. In addition, the stock market valuation incorporates assessments of strategic and financial risks taken to generate returns as well as the value of intangibles.

The disadvantages of the shareholder value maximization approach are that markets can be irrational, and managers may respond to fads instead of sound business logic to build unsustainable business models. There is no clarity on how micro decisions, such as setting up a new factory or introducing a relatively small new product, will impact stock market reaction. Nevertheless, firms like Amazon and Uber, which pursue this financial mindset, believe that markets will reward building dominant positions and profits will ultimately follow.

Of course, both companies in the future must be cognizant of the emerging stakeholder value creation model. Rather than give primacy to profits or shareholders, it attempts to balance the interests of different stakeholders, including customers, employees, suppliers and partners, community and shareholders. The challenge for the stakeholder value model is that it does not help managers with any analytical perspective on how to balance the interests of one stakeholder against the other. In the face of this ambiguity, when push comes to shove, managers fall back on implementing the traditional models of profits and shareholder value. Given their size, employee count and impact on society, Amazon and Walmart are going to be unable to escape greater scrutiny. They will have to be more vigilant to the interests of various competing stakeholders.

The Future is Retail Media

Walmart has been the largest company in the world in terms of revenues for more than two decades, having overtaken Exxon Mobil in 2001. While it took Walmart around forty years since it was founded to reach this position, it may take Amazon only thirty years. Going by its 2021 performance, 2023 may be the year when Amazon dethrones Walmart and claims the title for the first time. Or it may take a couple of more years to overtake Walmart. The big boost to online retail at the expense of offline in 2020–21 was because of the pandemic. In 2022, Amazon's revenues for its own online retail dipped as shoppers returned to the store. In contrast, Walmart grew its revenues in 2022 by 6.7 per cent. However, other parts of Amazon—AWS, Marketplace, advertising—are still demonstrating strong growth.

These are two exceptional companies. While Amazon is clearly perceived to be the online innovator and disruptor relative to established traditional brick-and-mortar Walmart, this view would benefit from some updating as this book argues. Until recently, Amazon and Walmart grew by staying in their own lanes—offline for Walmart and online for Amazon. Now, with their omnichannel models, they will have to confront each other directly. The challenge for Walmart is to change effectively for the e-commerce world while not forgetting the strength, attractiveness and continued value-creating potential of its physical store footprint.

Walmart, through its digital transformation, is emulating Amazon's business model. It is rapidly onboarding third parties on to its marketplace and has a new focus on retail media. To complement its assortment online, at the end of 2022, Walmart had 1,50,000 merchants on its platform.[5] While still small relative to the 2 million-plus sellers on Amazon, it has helped close the gap with Amazon with respect to online sales, and even slightly lead Amazon, albeit via acquisition, in India. In the last quarter of 2022, Walmart's e-commerce grew by 17 per cent while Amazon's declined by 2 per cent.[6] Walmart is clearly establishing itself as a worthy online, or at least an omnichannel, competitor to Amazon.

Retail-owned e-commerce sites are now generating $125 billion in advertising revenues.[7] By 2028, retail media is expected to surpass television media.[8] Retail media is the third wave of digital media after search and social. It is the fastest-growing portion of digital advertising spending. Whereas it took search fourteen years (2002–16) and social media eleven years (2008–19) to grow from $1 billion to over $30 billion in advertising, retail media made the same journey in five years (2016–21). Brands favour advertising on retailer websites as it reduces the power of the Google and Meta duopoly. The largest retailers with strong online sales are morphing into media companies.

For retailers like Walmart, this advertising is a double win as they not only make money from advertising but also from every product sold consequently. Profit margins for retailers on their media advertising sales can be 90 per cent. Compare that to the 25 per cent gross margin and 3 per cent net margin in the traditional Walmart retail model. In 2022, Walmart had revenues of $2.7 billion from advertising, still negligible compared to Amazon's $38 billion. However, a study indicated that Walmart advertising revenues, albeit from a much lower base, would grow by 42 per cent in 2023, compared to 19 per cent for Amazon, 5 per cent for Meta and 3 per cent for Google.[9] The Meta-Google duopoly has seen five years of declining combined market share from a peak of 54.7 per cent in 2017 to 48.4 per cent in 2022.[10] There is no doubt that there is a shift of ad dollars by brands to retailers from search and social. There is a blurring of industries in the war for customer data and eyeballs.

Both these behemoths are profitable and command large market capitalization, even if Amazon's current $1.5 trillion dwarfs Walmart's $420 billion. The founders of both companies have occupied the richest person in the world title at some stage. They are the largest private employers, with employee numbers exceeding 1.5 million at Amazon and 2 million at Walmart. While not known as great paymasters, the minimum hourly wage at Walmart and Amazon in the US is similar, around $17.50, as they compete in the same labour pool. Wages and initiatives to unionize workers have increased at both firms in recent years. While Amazon has always outperformed on the American Customer Satisfaction Index (2023 score is 84), Walmart has struggled on this front (2023 score is 70), at least in comparison to the sales it generates.[11]

As outlined in this book, both companies have built tremendous supply chain infrastructures, albeit for different purposes. Amazon is a world-class pioneer for small package picking and delivery to home. No one optimizes the home delivery system better or has allocated more money to resolving this problem, even if delivery is still a losing proposition. However, this is at the heart of Amazon's strategy of dominating online retail. Walmart has been a pioneer in redefining manufacturer-retailer relationships. Its supply chain is most efficient in managing the case logistics from suppliers to its distribution centres and then to more than 10,000 retail outlets.

In terms of sought-after generic competitive advantages, both firms elicit high brand trust, customer lock-in (customers unwilling or too satisfied to switch to or consider competitors), rational price discipline (neither firm exploits its dominant position to extract price premiums), innovative business models (that are difficult to copy and contrast with established industry practice), economies of scale (largest firms in the world) and scalability (ability to add customers at negligible marginal cost).

Arguably, the only missing generic competitive advantages in their business, primarily because they are retailers, are innovative products (though Amazon does have some, both have innovative processes) and unique resources (usually defined as access to raw materials but could be viewed as the supply chains they have built). It is not by chance that they are the two largest firms in the world.

With their enormous scale, both these firms are under the microscope for their impact on the environment. While Walmart has made progress on sustainability in recent years, the home delivery model of Amazon is not an environmentally-friendly one. With consumers demanding this convenience, it is hard to imagine substantial progress by Amazon on sustainability, especially in the face of continued growth.

Final Thoughts

In conclusion, omnichannel shopping seems to be taking Amazon and Walmart towards an inevitable clash as e-commerce accounts for an increasing share of retail. Yet, as explained in Chapter 4, everyone seems to shop at both, and the more appropriate question is for what needs does a shopper prefer Amazon or Walmart. This depends on the type of product (e.g., books versus groceries) and dominant need (convenience versus price). Despite the doom and gloom expressed for physical store formats, as demonstrated in Chapter 7, convenience stores, duty-free operators and first-price chains are thriving despite limited online offerings. This does not negate the need for other physical stores to evolve into delivering deep experiences that online stores cannot replicate.

In their quest to become omnichannel, Walmart has clearly demonstrated greater finesse in adopting online sales while Amazon has struggled with brick-and-mortar stores. Yet,

Walmart's online sales as per Chapters 5 and 6 are earnings-dilutive. To compensate for that as argued in this chapter, Walmart must push more aggressively into marketplace and advertising. In summary, we expect both these retailers to survive and thrive, pivoting their business models to emphasize advertising, while fulfilling complementary needs for shoppers.

It is not hyperbole to observe that these two companies have changed consumer behaviour, how brands are marketed and distributed, and transformed the retail industry in the process. No wonder they have been mainstays of teaching strategy, marketing and operations in business schools globally. Some may argue that being the benchmark for best business practices and innovation, Amazon and Walmart have changed the world despite each operating in only about twenty countries. Both these firms have in their DNA a restless dissatisfaction which drives them forward. Neither one is going to concede the marketplace to the other in their clash. Instead, they are going to coexist in strategic complementarity in the omnichannel world, with greater focus by each on what they do well versus the other. It will be fascinating to follow this clash of the giants.

Chapter Takeaways

- Amazon and Walmart are approaching retail from different strategic perspectives, business models and mindsets.
- Amazon's competence is exploration of new arenas for radical disruptive innovation. It is a safe place to fail. In contrast, Walmart has perfected the exploitation of a known landscape. It is a relentless executor of incremental innovation.
- Amazon was born as a platform, focused on building a network through large investments in infrastructure. Its competitive advantage is the size of the network and how

easy it makes it for players to transact with each other. As fixed costs are high but marginal costs are low, scale brings exponential increases in total profits. Walmart was conceived before we knew what platforms were. It follows the traditional product logic of making a profit on each sale and scale bringing linear increases in total profits.

- Walmart follows the profit maximization mindset, wishing to deliver consistent profit and dividend increases each year. Decisions are evaluated on profitability. Amazon follows a shareholder wealth maximization model, where decisions are based on achieving dominant positions in emerging industries. It has the mindset to tolerate years of losses in pursuit of this and to obtain the indulgence of its investors.
- The challenge of change is greater for Walmart as customer preferences migrate to online relative to offline retail. It has been slow off the mark but has now established itself as the strongest challenger to Amazon on e-commerce in the US. In contrast, Amazon has been less successful with physical stores. Both these giants need to pay attention to the emergence of social commerce, especially the parent company of TikTok.

Acknowledgements

First and foremost, I gratefully acknowledge the support of Singapore Management University (SMU) for this book. SMU has been my academic home since 2017 and the Lee Kong Chian Professorship has funded my research activities. Specifically, for this book, the professorship helped defray the travel expenses and pay for the research assistants. The financial support is made possible through the Lee Kong Chian Fund for Excellence, instituted by the Lee Foundation.

Professor Kapil Tuli, through the Centre for Retailing at SMU, generously provided the funding for the initial cases written on Amazon versus Walmart. The Centre for Management Practice at SMU, led by Havovi Joshi, facilitated this case-writing process with case writers and copy editors. Furthermore, at SMU, I would also like to acknowledge the gracious support of the deans (Bert De Reyck and Gerry George), faculty dean (Melyvn Teo), faculty assistant (Evelyn Lee), and my colleagues (especially Josephine Tan, Junqiu Jiang, Kapil Tuli and Sandeep Chandukala).

This book could not have been written without unstinting support in editing and research provided by Sheetal Mittal.

Sheetal and I started working together on cases when I first arrived at SMU. We co-authored cases on Gucci, Luckin versus Starbucks in China as well as Zara in China and India. More importantly, for the purposes of this book, we co-wrote two versions of the Amazon versus Walmart case with teaching notes in 2018 and 2022. Sheetal patiently helped collect all the information needed to facilitate the writing of the individual chapters and edited them. Sheetal is an amazing case writer and I am privileged that she continues to collaborate with me even after she departed from SMU for the USA.

Finally, my deepest acknowledgement to the wonderful Suseela Yesudian for her efforts on this and all my previous books. I can always count on her critical feedback. Without her, I am lost!

Notes

Chapter 1: Amazon and Walmart on a Collision Course

1. All $ currency is US$ unless otherwise specified.
2. Walmart 2022 Annual Report, https://s201.q4cdn.com/262069030/files/doc_downloads/LatestReports/WMT-FY2022-Annual-Report.pdf.
3. 'Quarterly Retail E-commerce Sales', US Census Bureau News, U.S. Department of Commerce, 2022, https://www.census.gov/retail/mrts/www/data/pdf/ec_current.pdf.
4. 'IGD: New US Grocery Forecasts Reveal $20bn Online Growth Opportunity', IGD, 5 October 2017, https://www.igd.com/About-us/Media/Press-releases-and-blogs/Press-release/t/igd-new-us-grocery-forecasts-reveal-20bn-online-growth-opportunity/i/17616.
5. Russell Redman, 'Amazon Go Draws High Interest from U.S. Shoppers', *Supermarket News*, 24 February 2021, https://www.supermarketnews.com/retail-financial/amazon-go-draws-high-interest-us-shoppers.
6. Phil Wahba, 'A Record 12,200 Stores Closed in 2020 as e-commerce, Pandemic Changed Retail Forever', *Fortune*, 7 January 2021, https://fortune.com/2021/01/07/record-store-closings-bankruptcy-2020/.
7. Lauren Thomas, 'UBS Expects 50,000 Store Closures in the U.S. over the Next 5 Years after Pandemic Pause', CNBC, 13 April 2022, https://www.cnbc.com/2022/04/13/ubs-50000-retail-store-closures-in-us-by-2026-after-pandemic-pause.html.

Chapter 2: Walmart: The Original Retail Disruptor

1. The diffusion of store openings radiating out from a central point (previous store) in all directions. With its stores close to each other, it allowed Walmart to facilitate and economize the logistics for shipments, for example, the optimal use of a single truck to make multiple deliveries, and to easily transfer experienced managers and other personnel from existing stores to the new stores.
2. Walmart Annual Report 2022.
3. Nirmalya Kumar, 'The Power of Trust in Manufacturer-Retailer Relationships', *Harvard Business Review*, 74 (November–December 1996), pp. 92–106.
4. Nirmalya Kumar, 'Kill a Brand, Keep a Customer', *Harvard Business Review*, 81 (December 2003), pp. 86–95.
5. Hayley Peterson, 'Walmart is Unleashing 2 Key Weapons against Amazon in 700 Stores', *Business Insider*, 5 April 2018, https://www.businessinsider.sg/walmart-online-pickup-tower-review-2017-8/?r=US&IR=T, accessed June 2022.
6. Tricia McKinnon, '6 Reasons Walmart's eCommerce Strategy Is Winning', Indigo Digital, 24 February 2022, https://www.indigo9digital.com/blog/4-secrets-to-walmarts-ecommerce-sucess#:~:text= . . . 20CEO, accessed June 2022.
7. Omer Riaz, 'The Benefits of Selling on Walmart Marketplace, and How to Get Started', *Forbes*, 3 January 2022, https://www.forbes.com/sites/forbesagencycouncil/2022/01/03/the-benefits-of-selling-on-walmart-marketplace-and-how-to-get-started/?sh=20dbbc0c7196, accessed June 2022.
8. Mike O'Brien, 'Walmart Gives Shopify's 1 Million+ Sellers Access to its Marketplace', Multichannel Merchant, 16 June 2020, https://multichannelmerchant.com/ecommerce/walmart-gives-shopifys-1-million-sellers-access-marketplace/, accessed February 2022.

Chapter 3: Amazon: The E-Commerce Pioneer

1. Amazon Annual Report 2018, https://s2.q4cdn.com/299287126/files/doc_financials/annual/2018-Annual-Report.pdf.
2. Simon Kemp, 'Digital in the United States: All the Statistics You Need In 2021', DataReportal, 9 February 2021, https://datareportal.com/reports/digital-2021-united-states-of-america.

3. Tracey Wallace, 'The Amazon Timeline: 20 Years And 18K% Increase In Sales', The BigCommerce Blog, 15 May 2017, https://www.bigcommerce.com/blog/amazon-timeline-infographic/.

4. Yaqub M., 'Amazon Third Party Seller Statistics: 2022 Edition', BusinessDIT, 26 August 2021, https://www.businessdit.com/amazon-third-party-seller-statistics/.

5. Samantha B. Gordon, 'Pros and Cons of Amazon Prime', Consumer Reports, 27 October 2022, https://www.consumerreports.org/online-shopping/pros-cons-amazon-prime-a7384439028/.

6. 'Amazon to Raise the Price of Prime for First Time since 2018', Markets Insider, 4 February 2022, https://markets.businessinsider.com/news/stocks/amazon-to-raise-the-price-of-prime-for-first-time-since-2018-11002150.

7. S. Ovide, 'Amazon Prime: Loved at Almost Any Price', the *New York Times*, 12 January 2022, https://www.nytimes.com/2022/01/12/technology/amazon-prime-price.html.

8. Nirmalya Kumar and Jan-Benedict E.M. Steenkamp, *Private Label Strategy: How to Meet the Store Brand Challenge* (Boston: Harvard Business Review Press, 2007).

9. Katie Tarasov, 'How Amazon's Big Private-Label Business Is Growing and Leaving Small Brands to Protect against Knockoffs', CNBC, 12 October 2022, https://www.cnbc.com/2022/10/12/amazons-growing-private-label-business-is-challenge-for-small-brands.html.

10. eMarketer Editors, 'Where Do US Consumers Begin Their Product Searches?', Insider Intelligence Trends, Forecasts & Statistics, 29 November 2020, https://www.insiderintelligence.com/content/where-do-us-consumers-begin-their-product-searches.

11. Geri Mileva, 'Amazon Ad Revenue Statistics That Will Blow Your Mind', Influencer Marketing Hub, 23 February 2022, https://influencermarketinghub.com/amazon-ad-revenue/.

12. Liz Young, 'AI Tapped to Weed Out Products That Are Damaged', the *Wall Street Journal*, 1 June 2023, B4.

13. '23 Lessons From Jeff Bezos' Annual Letters To Shareholders', https://www.inovaconsulting.com.br/wp-content/uploads/2020/05/23-Lessons-From-Jeff-Bezos%E2%80%99-Annual-Letters-To-Shareholders.pdf.

14. Jeffrey P. Bezos, 'Letter To Shareholders 1998', (n.d.), https://s2.q4cdn.com/299287126/files/doc_financials/annual/2018-Letter-to-Shareholders.pdf.

15. Jeff Cunningham, '21 Amazing Lessons from Amazon and CEO Jeff Bezos', Chief Executive, (n.d.), https://chiefexecutive.net/21-amazing-lessons-amazon-jeff-bezos/.

16. Jeffrey P. Bezos, 'Letter to Shareholders 2001', (n.d.), https://s2.q4cdn.com/299287126/files/doc_financials/annual/2001_shareholderLetter.pdf.

17. https://www.aboutamazon.com/news/company-news/2017-letter-to-shareholders.

18. Russell Redman, 'Amazon Go Draws High Interest from U.S. Shoppers', Supermarket News, 24 February 2021, https://www.supermarketnews.com/retail-financial/amazon-go-draws-high-interest-us-shoppers.

19. Ben Fox Rubin, 'Amazon Shuttering Its Pop-up Kiosks across the US', CNET, 6 March 2019, https://www.cnet.com/tech/services-and-software/amazon-shuttering-its-pop-up-kiosks-across-the-us/.

20. 'Amazon and Whole Foods Market Announce Acquisition to Close This Monday, Will Work Together to Make High-Quality, Natural and Organic Food Affordable for Everyone', Business Wire, 24 August 2017, https://www.businesswire.com/news/home/20170824006124/en/Amazon-and-Whole-Foods-Market-Announce-Acquisition-to-Close-This-Monday-Will-Work-Together-to-Make-High-Quality-Natural-and-Organic-Food-Affordable-for-Everyone.

21. Russell Redman, 'Amazon Go Draws High Interest From U.S. Shoppers', Supermarket News.

22. Jon Springer, 'Amazon's Whole Food Vision: "Affordable for Everyone"', Supermarket News, 24 August 2017, https://www.supermarketnews.com/news/amazon-s-whole-foods-vision-affordable-everyone.

23. Jeffrey P. Bezos, '2016 Letter to Shareholders', Amazon News, 17 April 2017, https://www.aboutamazon.com/news/company-news/2016-letter-to-shareholders.

24. Russell Redman, 'Amazon Go Draws High Interest From U.S. Shoppers', Supermarket News.

Chapter 4: The Battle for Customers

1. Nirmalya Kumar, *Marketing as Strategy: Understanding the CEO's Agenda for Driving Growth and Innovation* (Boston: Harvard Business School Press, 2004).

2. M. Hanbury, 'The Average Amazon Shopper Still Earns More than Walmart's, and It Reveals a Key Challenge for the E-commerce Giant', Business Insider, 25 January 2020, https://www.businessinsider.com/amazon-shoppers-richer-than-walmart-2020-1.

3. D. Reuter, 'Meet the Typical Walmart Shopper, a 59-Year-Old White Suburban Woman Earning $80,000 a Year', Business Insider, 31 January 2023, https://www.businessinsider.com/typical-walmart-shopper-demographic-white-woman-earning-middle-income-2021-7.

4. D. Reuter, 'Meet The Typical Amazon Customer, a College-Educated Married Woman in the Southeast Earning $80,000', Business Insider, 4 February 2023, https://www.businessinsider.com/typical-amazon-shopper-demographic-educated-woman-earning-middle-income-2021-7.

5. W.C. Kim and R. Mauborgne, 'Value Innovation: The Strategic Logic of High Growth', *Harvard Business Review* (July 2004), https://hbr.org/2004/07/value-innovation-the-strategic-logic-of-high-growth.

6. M. Vanegas, 'Walmart Vs. Amazon: Who Has Cheaper Prices In 2018?', LendEDU, 6 April 2020, https://lendedu.com/blog/walmart-vs-amazon/.

7. K. Souza, 'Amazon Again Edges Out Walmart as Lowest Cost Online Retailer', Talk Business & Politics, 30 November 2022, https://talkbusiness.net/2022/11/amazon-again-edges-out-walmart-as-lowest-cost-online-retailer/.

8. M. Pasquali, 'U.S. E-commerce Categories by Retail Share 2021', Statista, 20 October 2022, https://www.statista.com/statistics/203043/online-share-of-total-us-retail-revenue-projection/.

9. B. Droesch, 'US E-commerce by Category 2021', Insider Intelligence Trends, Forecasts & Statistics, 27 April 2021, https://www.insiderintelligence.com/content/us-ecommerce-by-category-202.1.

10. M. Djordjevic, '25 Awe-Inspiring Apparel Industry Statistics [The 2021 Edition]', SaveMyCent, 11 February 2021, https://savemycent.com/apparel-industry-statistics/.

11. R. Redman, 'E-commerce to Account for 20% of U.S. Grocery Market by 2026', Supermarket News, 22 October 2021, https://www.supermarketnews.com/online-retail/e-commerce-account-20-us-grocery-market-2026.

12. A. Nicolaou and L. Hook, 'Now Amazon Is Disrupting Fashion Retail, Too', *Financial Times*, 26 January 2018.

13. M. Pinola, 'Find Out Which Clothing Brands Run Too Big or Small with This Chart', Lifehacker, 19 August 2019, https://lifehacker.com/find-out-which-clothing-brands-run-too-big-or-small-wit-1668791215.

14. https://www.shopify.com/sg/enterprise/ecommerce-returns.

15. L. Valdellon, 'Must-Know Ecommerce Return Rate Statistics and Trends In 2021', CleverTap, (n.d.), https://clevertap.com/blog/ecommerce-return-rate-statistics/, retrieved 5 February 2023.

16. K. Saleh, 'E-commerce Product Return Rate – Statistics and Trends [Infographic]', Invesp, 5 April 2016, https://www.invespcro.com/blog/ecommerce-product-return-rate-statistics/.

17. G. Swan, 'Everything You Need to Know about Amazon Apparel', Tinuiti, 12 June 2019, https://tinuiti.com/blog/amazon/amazon-apparel/.

18. James Melton, 'Online Grocery Sales More Than Double in 2020', Digital Commerce 360, 5 November 2021, https://www.digitalcommerce360.com/article/online-food-report/, accessed 5 February 2023.

19. April Berthene, 'Ecommerce Is 46.0% of All Apparel Sale', Digital Commerce 360, 28 June 2021, https://www.digitalcommerce360.com/article/online-apparel-sales-us/, accessed 5 February 2023.

Chapter 5: Is Online Retailing Profitable?

1. M. P. McNair, *Significant Trends and Developments in the Postwar Period, in Competitive Distribution in a Free High-Level Economy and Its Implications for the University* (Pittsburgh: University of Pittsburgh Press, 1958), pp. 1–25.

2. J-B. E. M. Steenkamp and N. Kumar, 'Don't Be Undersold!', *Harvard Business Review*, 87 (December 2009), pp. 90–95.

3. Nirmalya Kumar, *Marketing as Strategy: Understanding the CEO's Agenda for Driving Growth and Innovation* (Boston: Harvard Business School Press, 2004).

4. Jacques Horovitz and Nirmalya Kumar, *Amazon: Success, Survival, or Suicide* (IMD Case GM922, 2001).

5. 'Jeff Bezos' Risky Bet', *Businessweek*, 3 November 2006, https://www.nbcnews.com/id/wbna15536386.

6. Karen Weise, 'Amazon's Profit Falls Sharply as Company Buys Growth', the *New York Times*, 24 October 2019, https://www.nytimes.com/2019/10/24/technology/amazon-earnings.html.

7.   'List of Countries by GDP (nominal)', https://en.wikipedia.org/wiki/
     List_of_countries_by_GDP_(nominal).

8.   James Melton, 'Fast Grocery Delivery Can Win Customer Loyalty,
     but Executing on It Can Be Costly', Digital Commerce 360, 11
     January 2019, https://www.digitalcommerce360.com/2019/01/11/
     fast-delivery-can-win-loyalty-for-grocery-retailer-but-costs-are-
     unsustainable/.

9.   Sam Silverstein, 'Online Grocery Reaches New Heights in April',
     Grocery Dive, 29 April 2020, https://www.grocerydive.com/news/
     online-grocery-reaches-new-heights-in-april/576993/, accessed June
     2022.

10. Vishwa Chandra et al., 'Achieving Profitable Online Grocery Order
     Fulfilment', McKinsey & Company, 18 May 2022, https://www.
     mckinsey.com/industries/retail/our-insights/achieving-profitable-
     online-grocery-order-fulfillment, accessed June 2022.

11. James Melton, 'Fast Grocery Delivery Can Win Customer Loyalty,
     but Executing on It Can Be Costly', Digital Commerce 360.

12. Jonathan Eley and Ryan McMorrow, 'Why Supermarkets Are
     Struggling to Profit from the Online Grocery Boom', the *Financial
     Times*, 23 July 2020, https://www.ft.com/content/b985249c-1ca1-
     41a8-96b5-0adcc889d57d.

13. https://www.statista.com/statistics/1178365/online-grocery-profit-
     margin-worldwide/.

14. John Matarese, 'Walmart.com Online Prices May be Higher Than In-
     Store', WCPO, 9 November 2017, https://www.wcpo.com/money/
     consumer/dont-waste-your-money/walmartcom-online-prices-may-
     be-higher-than-in-store, accessed July 2018.

15. Dark store refers to a retail or distribution centre that caters
     exclusively to online shopping.

16. eMarketer Editors, 'Do Most Searches Really Start on Amazon?',
     Insider Intelligence, 7 January 2020, https://www.insiderintelligence.
     com/content/do-most-searchers-really-start-on-amazon.

Chapter 6: The Last-Mile Challenge

1.   'Inside the Economics of 10-Minute Grocery Delivery Startups,
     Which Eke Out Higher Margins with Pricier Convenience Store
     Goods and Less Choice', Bain & Company, 14 April 2021, https://

www.bain.com/about/media-center/bain-in-the-news/2021/inside-the-economics-of-10-minute-grocery-delivery-startups-which-eke-out-higher-margins-with-pricier-convenience-store-goods-and-less-choice/.

2. Greg Bensinger, 'Amazon's New Secret Weapon: Delivery Lockers', the *Wall Street Journal*, 7 August 2021, https://www.wsj.com/articles/SB10000872396390443545504577567763829784538.

3. Heather Reinblatt, 'Amazon Lockers: Everything You Need to Know to Start Using Them Today', Circuit, 17 November 2022, https://getcircuit.com/package-tracker/blog/how-do-amazon-lockers-work.

4. Amazon Press Room, 'Amazon Key Features—Keyless Entry, Guest Access, and Ability to Monitor and Lock/Unlock Your Door from Anywhere—Now Available Nationwide', Business Wire, 5 April 2018, http://phx.corporate-ir.net/phoenix.zhtml?c=176060&p=irol-newsArticle&ID=2341237, accessed June 2018.

5. Isobel Asher Hamilton, 'Amazon Is Offering Building Managers $100 Gift Cards as an Incentive to Install "Key" Devices, Which Let Delivery Drivers Get into the Lobby at All Hours', Insider, 26 July 2021, https://www.businessinsider.com/amazon-key-for-business-delivery-drivers-packages-building-managers-2021-7, accessed June 2022.

6. Steve Banker, 'Amazon Supply Chain Innovation Continues', *Forbes*, 1 April 2021, https://www.forbes.com/sites/stevebanker/2021/04/01/amazon-supply-chain-innovation-continues/?sh=20dee95977e6, accessed June 2022.

7. Spencer Soper and Natalie Wong, 'Amazon Builds Property Empire, Quietly Buying Land Across the US', Bloomberg, 13 June 2022, https://www.bloomberg.com/news/features/2022-06-13/amazon-builds-property-empire-for-warehouses-even-as-online-sales-growth-slows#xj4y7vzkg.

8. 'Amazon Global Supply Chain and Fulfillment Center Network', MWPVL, https://www.mwpvl.com/html/amazon_com.html; Tara Johnson, 'Amazon Fulfillment Center Locations: The Ultimate List', tinuiti, 23 August 2022, https://tinuiti.com/blog/amazon/amazon-fulfillment-centers-map/.

9. Jeffrey Dastin, 'Amazon to Spend $1.49 Billion on Air Cargo Hub, Fans Talk of Bigger Ambitions', Reuters, 1 February 2017, https://www.reuters.com/article/us-amazon-com-shipping/amazon-to-

spend-1-49-billion-on-air-cargo-hub-fans-talk-of-bigger-ambitions-idUSKBN15G3GI, accessed May 2018.

10. Kirsten Korosec, 'Amazon's $1.5 Billion Us Air Cargo Hub Is Open for Business', techcrunch, 11 August 2021, https://techcrunch.com/2021/08/11/amazons-1-5-billion-u-s-air-cargo-hub-is-open-for-business/, accessed June 2022.

11. Katie Tarasov, 'Amazon Is Now Shipping Cargo for outside Customers in Its Latest Move to Compete with FedEx and UPS', CNBC, 4 September 2021, https://www.cnbc.com/2021/09/04/how-amazon-is-shipping-for-third-parties-to-compete-with-fedex-and-ups.html#:~:text=Seven%20years%20and%2010%20billion,of%20more%20than%2070%20planes.

12. 'Amazon Is a Logistics Beast – A Detailed Teardown', Platform Revolution (n.d.) https://platformthinkinglabs.com/materials/amazon-is-a-logistics-beast-a-detailed-teardown/.

13. Tricia McKinnon, 'Why DoorDash & Other Delivery Apps Struggle with Profitability', 17 January 2023, https://www.indigo9digital.com/blog/fooddeliveryappprofitability.

14. Jessica Bursztynsky, 'Doordash Sues New York City over New Data-Sharing Law', CNBC, 15 September 2021, https://www.cnbc.com/2021/09/15/doordash-sues-new-york-city-over-new-data-sharing-law.html.

15. Marcin Zgola, 'Will the Gig Economy Become the New Working-Class Norm?', Forbes, 12 August 2021, https://www.forbes.com/sites/forbesbusinesscouncil/2021/08/12/will-the-gig-economy-become-the-new-working-class-norm/?sh=7bf169abaee6.

16. Sarah Butler, 'Uber Drivers Entitled to Workers' Rights, UK Supreme Court Rules', the Guardian, 19 February 2021, https://www.theguardian.com/technology/2021/feb/19/uber-drivers-workers-uk-supreme-court-rules-rights.

17. Zane McNeill, '"A Huge Loss for Workers": CA Court Rules that Gig Workers Are Contractors', Truthout, 17 March 2023, https://truthout.org/articles/ca-court-rules-that-gig-workers-are-not-employees-in-loss-for-workers/.

18. The Associated Press, 'Spain Hits Delivery App with New Fine for Labor Violation', ABC News, 24 January 2023, https://abcnews.go.com/Business/wireStory/spain-hits-delivery-app-new-fine-labor-violation-96629948#:~:text=MADRID%20%2D%2D%20

Spain's%20labor%20ministry,irregular%20immigrants%20 without%20work%20permits.

19. Natasha Lomas, 'Delivery Hero Calls Last Orders on Foodpanda in Germany, Japan as It Tightens Focus On Q-Commerce and Logistics-as-a-Service', TechCrunch, 22 December 2021, https://techcrunch. com/2021/12/22/delivery-hero-exits-germany-japan/.

20. 'Real Income of Food Delivery Workers Drops as Prices Rise', https://www.moneycontrol.com/news/business/startup/real-income-of-food-delivery-workers-drops-as-prices-rise-11277701. html.

21. Dearbail Jordan and Zoe Conway, 'Amazon Strikes: Workers Claim Their Toilet Breaks Are Timed', BBC News, 25 January 2023, https:// www.bbc.com/news/business-64384287.

22. Preetika Rana, 'What Happened When Uber's CEO Started Driving for Uber', the *Wall Street Journal*, 7 April 2023, https://www.wsj. com/articles/uber-ceo-started-driving-for-uber-5bef5023.

23. Kaycee Encrva, 'Consumers Generate 10KG of Single-Use Plastic Waste in Food Deliveries Every Year', Viable.Earth, 3 March 2022, https://viable.earth/plant-based-food/consumers-generate-10kg-of-single-use-plastic-waste-in-food-deliveries-every-year/ #:~:text=The%20agency%20based%20its%20calculations,10.8%20 kilograms%20of%20plastic%20waste.

24. Ibid.

25. Changeadmin, 'Food Delivery Companies Trying to Reduce Plastic Waste', ChangeStarted, 2 September 2021, https://changestarted. com/food-delivery-companies-trying-to-reduce-plastic-waste/.

Chapter 7: Strategies for Brick-and-Mortar Stores

1. NCSolution Survey, 'Convenience Stores Offer Destination for Product, Brand Discovery', Supermarket News, 3 November 2022, https://www.supermarketnews.com/consumer-trends/convenience-stores-offer-destination-product-brand-discovery.

2. Ibid.

3. 'Convenience Stores and Their Communities', NACS (n.d.), https:// www.convenience.org/Topics/Community/Convenience-Stores-and-Their-Communities.

4. Ibid.

5. NCSolution Survey, 'Convenience Stores Offer Destination for Product, Brand Discovery', Supermarket News.

6. Ibid.

7. Market Analysis Report, 'Convenience Stores Market Size, Share & Trends Analysis Report By Type (Cigarettes & Tobacco, Foodservice, Packaged Beverages, Center Store, Low Alcoholic Beverages), By Region, And Segment Forecasts, 2022 – 2028', Grand View Research (n.d.), https://www.grandviewresearch.com/industry-analysis/convenience-stores-market-report#.

8. Erick Burgueño Salas, 'Coronavirus: Impact on the Aviation Industry Worldwide - Statistics & Facts', Statista, 17 January 2023, https://www.statista.com/topics/6178/coronavirus-impact-on-the-aviation-industry-worldwide/#topicOverview.

9. Nirmalya Kumar and Lipika Bhattacharya, 'Toblerone Pricing at Airport Duty Free', 2023 SMU case #SMU-23-0019.

10. Research Dive, 'Global Duty-Free Retailing Market Expected to Grow at 10.6% CAGR and Garner $94,203.7 Million in the 2022-2031 Timeframe', 20 December 2022, https://www.globenewswire.com/en/news-release/2022/12/20/2577157/0/en/Global-Duty-Free-Retailing-Market-Expected-to-Grow-at-10-6-CAGR-and-Garner-94-203-7-Million-in-the-2022-2031-Timeframe-240-Pages-Announced-by-Research-Dive.html.

11. Alex Foy, 'Captive Audience', Pragma (n.d.), https://pragmagroup.com/insights-news/2022/05/21/captive-audience.

12. Samantha Shankman, 'Luxury Brands Are Bullish on the Future of Airport Retail', Skift, 6 June 2017, https://skift.com/2017/06/06/luxury-brands-are-bullish-on-the-future-of-airport-retail/.

13. 'Why Do Some Offline Stores Sell Products Cheaper than Online Stores?', https://www.quora.com/Why-do-some-offline-stores-sell-products-cheaper-than-online-stores.

14. Alberto Cavallo, 'Are Online and Offline Prices Similar? Evidence from Large Multi-Channel Retailers', American Economic Review, 107-1 (January 2017), https://www.hbs.edu/ris/Publication%20Files/Cavallo_Alberto_J6_Are%20Online%20and%20Offline%20Prices%20Similar_2a1a63af-8938-4680-bb23-a850324b096a.pdf.

15. nhavale, 'A Detail Price Comparison: Offline/Online Grocery Store', DesiDime, 3 August 2020, https://www.desidime.com/discussions/a-detail-price-comparison-offline-online-grocery-store.

16. Paul Davidson, 'Cheaper Online or at the Store? Heading to a Store May Save Money', *USA Today*, 22 April 2019, https://www.usatoday.com/story/money/2019/04/22/best-budget-strategy-cheaper-shop-store-online/3507722002/.

17. Francesca Nicasio, '10 Types of Retail Experiences That Keep Customers Coming Back', Vend, 4 May 2021, https://www.vendhq.com/blog/retail-experience/.

18. Grace Dean, 'Here's Everything You Need to Know About Lidl, the German Discount Chain That's Struggling to Keep Up with Aldi's Rapid US Growth', Insider, 4 June 2023, https://www.businessinsider.com/lidl-history-size-store-count-us-growth-supermarket-german-discounter-2022-12#lidl-now-has-more-than-12000-storesacross-31-countries-6.

19. Abbas Haleem, 'Costco Ecommerce Sales Drop; Net Sales Still Increase 1.9%', 1 June 2023, https://www.digitalcommerce360.com/2023/06/01/costco-ecommerce-sales/.

20. Tricia McKinnon, 'Ecommerce and Its Profitability Issue. Why It's So Hard to Make Money', Indigo Digital, 11 January 2023, https://www.indigo9digital.com/blog/ecommerceprofitability.

21. 'All US Outlet Malls', Outlet Stores Malls (n.d.), https://www.outletstoresmalls.com/outlet-malls/all-us.

22. Joanne Shurvell, 'Luxury Shopping Destination Bicester Village Offers Major Fashion Discounts and a Great Day Out', Forbes, 30 April 2019, https://www.forbes.com/sites/joanneshurvell/2019/04/30/top-uk-tourist-attraction-bicester-village-offers-fashion-discounts-and-a-great-day-out/?sh=fc0a948eee53.

23. Guang Chen, Zi Chen, Steve Saxon and Jackey Yu, 'Outlook for China Tourism 2023: Light at the End of the Tunnel', McKinsey & Company, 9 May 2023, https://www.mckinsey.com/industries/travel-logistics-and-infrastructure/our-insights/outlook-for-china-tourism-2023-light-at-the-end-of-the-tunnel.

24. 'The Best Shopping Tourism Country in the World', Arab Travelers (n.d.), https://en.arabtravelers.com/the-best-shopping-tourism-country-in-the-world/.

25. Ibid.

26. Larry Bleiberg, 'Let's Go to the Mall: 10 Shopping Centers That Are Tourist Destinations in Their Own Right', *USA Today Travel*, 16 November 2019, https://www.usatoday.com/story/travel/desti

nations/10greatplaces/2019/11/16/10-great-malls-tourist-that-are-destinations-on-their-own/4203187002/

27. Ibid.

28. Ibid.

29. Ibid.

30. Stewart Rubin, 'Challenges Confronting Regional Malls Intensify', New York Life, May 2017, https://www.newyorklife.com/assets/docs/pdfs/rei/Challenges-Confronting-Regional-Malls-Intensify.pdf.

31. Hannah Aster, 'Why Are Malls Dying in the US', 24 August 2023, https://www.shortform.com/blog/why-are-malls-dying/.

32. Candace Davison, 'If Malls Are Dying, Why Are We Still So Obsessed With Them?', https://www.purewow.com/family/are-malls-dying.

33. Eva Rothenberg, 'The US Mall Is Not Dying', 20 August 2023, https://edition.cnn.com/2023/08/20/business/shopping-mall-retail-growth/index.html.

34. Ibid.

35. Ezra Klein, 'How Barnes & Noble Came Back from Near Death', New York Times, 28 January 2023, https://www.nytimes.com/2023/01/28/opinion/barnes-noble-amazon-bookstore.html.

36. Jonathan Z. Zhang, Chun-Wei Chang, and Scott A. Neslin, 'How Physical Stores Enhance Customer Value: The Importance of Product Inspection Depth', Journal of Marketing, Volume 86, Issue 2 (7 April 2021), https://journals.sagepub.com/doi/10.1177/00222429211012106.

37. Jonathan Zhang and Scott Neslin, 'Leveraging the Physical Store to Boost Customer Value – Providing the Right Engagement at the Right Time', California Management Review, 24 June 2021, https://cmr.berkeley.edu/2021/06/leveraging-the-physical-store-to-boost-customer-value/.

38. Tricia McKinnon and Ben Rudolph, '14 Examples of Great Customer Experiences in Retail', Indigo Digital, 27 February 2023, https://www.indigo9digital.com/blog/topcustomerexperiences.

39. Ibid.

40. Ibid.

41. Bobby Marhamat, '11 Brands Winning with Memorable In-Store Experiences', Retail Customer Experience, 23 August 2022, https://www.retailcustomerexperience.com/blogs/11-brands-winning-with-memorable-in-store-experiences/.

42. Ibid.

43. Matthew Kish, 'Nike and Lululemon Are Obliterating the Competition When It Comes to Drawing Customers to Stores', Business Insider India, 18 March 2023, https://www.businessinsider.in/retail/news/nike-and-lululemon-are-obliterating-the-competition-when-it-comes-to-drawing-customers-to-stores/articleshow/98741571.cms.

44. Francesca Nicasio, '10 Types of Retail Experiences That Keep Customers Coming Back', Vend, 4 May 2021, https://www.vendhq.com/blog/retail-experience/.

45. 'Apple's Customer Experience Strategy: Turn Stores into "Town Squares"', Future Store Seattle 2023, https://futurestores.wbresearch.com/blog/apple-store-town-square-customer-experience.

46. Ibid.

47. Dave Bruno, 'Twenty Years Later: Four Things Retailers Can Learn From Apple's Entry in Retail', Chain Store Age, 23 May 2021, https://chainstoreage.com/twenty-years-later-four-things-retailers-can-learn-apples-entry-retail.

48. T. Ozbun, 'Walmart: eCommerce Sales Worldwide FY2019-FY2023, by Division', Statista, 20 March 2023, https://www.statista.com/statistics/1109330/walmart-ecommerce-sales-by-division-worldwide/.

49. Emma Sopadjieva, Utpal M. Dholakia and Beth Benjamin, 'A Study of 46,000 Shoppers Shows That Omnichannel Retailing Works', *Harvard Business Review*, 3 January 2017, https://hbr.org/2017/01/a-study-of-46000-shoppers-shows-that-omnichannel-retailing-works.

50. Fabio Devin, 'Amazing CX: Jumbo Creates Slow Checkout Lanes', dorve, 13 January 2023, https://dorve.com/blog/ux-news-articles-archive/cx-jumbo-slow-checkout/#:~:text=Jumbo%20Supermarket%2C%20a%20Dutch%20grocery,to%20chat%20with%20the%20cashier.

51. Nicholas Kristof, 'We Know the Cure for Loneliness. So Why Do We Suffer?', the *New York Times*, 6 September 2023, https://www.nytimes.com/2023/09/06/opinion/loneliness-epidemic-solutions.html?.

52. Fiona Zeng Skovhøj, 'Research Online Purchase Offline: What Does ROPO Mean to Your Business?', clerk.io, 22 February 2022, https://www.clerk.io/blog/research-online-purchase-offline.

53. Sandy Skrovan, 'Why Many Shoppers Go to Stores before Buying Online', RetailDive, 26 April 2017, https://www.retaildive.com/news/why-many-shoppers-go-to-stores-before-buying-online/441112/.

54. https://etailwest.wbresearch.com/blog/the-home-depots-ecommerce-strategy-for-omnichannel-personalization.

Chapter 8: The Clash for the Future in India

1. Tom Hancock, 'IKEA Assembles $1.4bn China Expansion Drive', *Financial Times*, 22 September 2019, https://www.ft.com/content/9d49a782-dae7-11e9-8f9b-77216ebe1f17.

2. Katya Naidu, 'Brick and Mortar Retailers Are Growing and Fuelling E-retail Growth Too', Business Insider India, 24 August 2022, https://www.businessinsider.in/business/news/brick-and-mortar-retailers-are-growing-and-fuelling-e-retail-growth-too/articleshow/93749847.cms.

3. Business Desk, 'Radhakrishna Damani's DMart Eyes Five Fold Expansion; Know Details', News 18, 18 August 2022, https://www.news18.com/news/business/radhakrishna-damanis-dmart-eyes-five-fold-expansion-know-details-5774467.html.

4. Vidya S, 'Mukesh Ambani-Backed Reliance Retail's Net Profit Jumps 30% to Rs 9,181 CR in FY23 on Higher Footfalls at Stores', *Business Today*, 21 April 2023, https://www.businesstoday.in/latest/corporate/story/mukesh-ambani-backed-reliance-retails-net-profit-jumps-30-to-rs-9181-cr-in-fy23-on-higher-footfalls-at-stores-378402-2023-04-21.

5. Indrajit Gupta, 'Noel Tata's Brahmastra', Founding Fuel, 28 August 2023, https://www.foundingfuel.com/column/strategic-intent/noel-tatas-brahmastra/.

6. Kelly Dawson, 'JD.ID Explores Omni-channel Innovation as Indonesia Warms to E-Commerce', 26 August 2021, https://jdcorporateblog.com/jd-id-explores-omni-channel-innovation-as-indonesia-warms-to-e-commerce/.

7. Petaling Jaya, 'Retailers See Revenue from Physical Stores to Rise', the *Star*, 3 August 2022, https://www.thestar.com.my/business/business-news/2022/08/03/retailers-see-revenue-from-physical-stores-to-rise.

8. Hoornweg and Pope, 'City Population 2025', Ontario Tech University, GCIF Working Paper No.4, https://sites.ontariotechu.ca/

sustainabilitytoday/urban-and-energy-systems/Worlds-largest-cities/population-projections/city-population-2025.php.

9. A. Minhas, 'E-commerce Market Value India 2014-2030', Statista, 5 January 2023, https://www.statista.com/statistics/792047/india-e-commerce-market-size/.

10. Anwesha Madhukalya, 'India Has the Third-Largest Online Shopper Base Globally; To Overtake US in 1-2 Yrs: Bain & Co', *Business Today*, 12 October 2022, https://www.businesstoday.in/latest/economy/story/india-has-the-third-largest-online-shopper-base-globally-to-overtake-us-in-1-2-yrs-bain-co-349631-2022-10-12.

11. SNS, 'Flipkart Group Buys Walmart India's Best Price, Launches Wholesale', the *Statesman*, 23 July 2020, https://www.thestatesman.com/business/flipkart-group-buys-walmart-indias-best-price-launches-wholesale-1502910830.html#.

12. Vijay Govindarajan and Anita Warren, 'How Amazon Adapted Its Business Model to India', *Harvard Business Review*, 20 July 2016, https://hbr.org/2016/07/how-amazon-adapted-its-business-model-to-india, accessed September 2018.

13. Isabelle Crossley, 'Amazon Retail India Plans to Open in 60 Tier 2 and 3 Cities', Fashion Network, 24 April 2019, https://in.fashionnetwork.com/news/Amazon-retail-india-plans-to-open-in-60-tier-2-and-3-cities,1092338.html.

14. Ibid.

15. Manish Singh, 'Amazon Launches "Smart Stores" in India to Win Mom and Pop', TechCrunch, 26 June 2020, https://techcrunch.com/2020/06/26/amazon-launches-smart-stores-in-india-to-win-mom-and-pop/?.

16. Indian Retailer Bureau, 'How E-Commerce has Evolved in India', IndianRetailer.com, 9 January 2023, https://www.indianretailer.com/article/technology-e-commerce/retail-trends/how-e-commerce-has-evolved-india#:~:text=The%20largest%20category%20on%20Amazon,year%2Don%2Dyear%20jump.

17. Ibid.

18. Jai Vardhan and Kunal Manchanda, 'Amazon Indian Ecosystem in FY22: $5.56 Bn Income and $834 Mn Loss', ENTRACKER, 19 September 2022, https://entrackr.com/2022/09/amazon-indian-ecosystem-in-fy22-5-56-bn-income-and-834-mn-loss/.

19. Spandan Sharma, 'A Success Story 10 Years in the Making: Key Milestones from the Flipkart Journey', Your Story, 9 May 2018, https://yourstory.com/2018/05/flipkart-through-the-years/, accessed September 2018.

20. Tricia McKinnon, 'What You Need to Know About Flipkart's Strategy', Indigo Digital, 21 April 2022, https://www.indigo9digital.com/blog/flipkartstrategy.

21. PTI, 'Flipkart Losses Widened to over Rs 7,800 Crore in FY22', the *Economic Times*, 7 November 2022, https://economictimes.indiatimes.com/markets/stocks/earnings/flipkart-losses-widened-to-over-rs-7800-crore-in-fy22/articleshow/95361053.cms?from=mdr.

22. PTI, 'Walmart Not Keen to Open Retail Stores in India; To Focus On Flipkart, PhonePe', the *Economic Times*, 11 March 2022, https://economictimes.indiatimes.com/industry/services/retail/walmart-not-keen-to-open-retail-stores-in-india-to-focus-on-flipkart-phonepe/articleshow/90155068.cms?from=mdr.

23. Digbijay Mishra, 'ETtech Exclusive: Accel, Tiger Global May Exit Flipkart in $1.5B Share Sale', the *Economic Times*, 26 January 2023, https://economictimes.indiatimes.com/tech/technology/exclusive-accel-tiger-global-may-exit-flipkart-in-1-5b-share-sale/articleshow/97326733.cms?from=mdr.

24. Mihir Dalal, 'Inside Flipkart, the Indian Giant Beating Amazon', rest of world, 14 February 2023, https://restofworld.org/2023/flipkart-walmart-india/.

25. Niharika Sharma, 'Amazon's $13 Billion Cloud Services Investment Is Its Largest-Ever in India', Quartz, 18 May 2023, https://stocks.apple.com/AM3asgIc0R5eurC5EV56ZXA.

Chapter 9: Incumbents versus Disruptors

1. 'Here Are 60 of Amazon's Biggest Failures Up to 2023', Failory, 24 January 2023, https://www.failory.com/blog/amazon-failures.

2. Brad Power and Ric Merrifield, 'Too Much Profit Can Doom Your Company', *Harvard Business Review*, June 2015, https://hbr.org/2015/06/too-much-profit-can-doom-your-company.

3. Milton Friedman, 'A Friedman Doctrine: The Social Responsibility of Business Is to Increase Its Profits', the *New York Times*, 13

September 1970, https://www.nytimes.com/1970/09/13/archives/a-friedman-doctrine-the-social-responsibility-of-business-is-to.html.

4. Alfred Rappaport, 'Selecting Strategies That Create Shareholder Value', *Harvard Business Review*, May 1981, https://hbr.org/1981/05/selecting-strategies-that-create-shareholder-value; Michael C. Jensen and Kevin J. Murphy, 'CEO Incentives—It's Not How Much You Pay, But How', *Harvard Business Review*, May–June 1990, https://hbr.org/1990/05/ceo-incentives-its-not-how-much-you-pay-but-how?autocomplete=true.

5. Gary Drenik, 'Walmart V. Amazon: Advertising, Inflation, and the Battle for Ecommerce Brands', *Forbes*, 3 March 2023, https://www.forbes.com/sites/garydrenik/2023/03/13/walmart-v-amazon-advertising-inflation-and-the-battle-for-ecommerce-brands/?sh=51f3ec4452b8.

6. Ibid.

7. James Davey, 'Retail Media Ad Revenue Forecast to Surpass TV by 2028', https://www.reuters.com/business/retail-consumer/retail-media-ad-revenue-forecast-surpass-tv-by-2028-2023-06-12/#.

8. Ibid.

9. 'Tech, Retail, and Streaming Companies Make Stronger Play for Digital Ad Dollars in 2023', 19 December 2022, https://www.insiderintelligence.com/content/tech-retail-streaming-companies-make-stronger-play-digital-ad-dollars-2023.

10. Patrick McGee, 'Meta and Alphabet Lose Dominance over the US Digital Ads Market', *Financial Times*, 23 December 2022, https://www.ft.com/content/4ff64604-a421-422c-9239-0ca8e5133042.

11. 'General Merchandise Retailers', American Satisfaction Index, 2023, https://www.theacsi.org/industries/retail/general-merchandise-retailers/.

Scan QR code to access the
Penguin Random House India website